Multi-Congregation Ministry

Multi-Congregation Ministry

Theology and Practice in a Changing Church

Malcolm Grundy

CANTERBURY
PRESS

Norwich

© Malcolm Grundy 2015

First published in 2015 by the Canterbury Press Norwich
Editorial Office
3rd Floor, Invicta House,
108–114 Golden Lane
London EC1Y 0TG, UK

Canterbury Press is an imprint of Hymns Ancient & Modern Ltd
(a registered charity)
13A Hellesdon Park Road, Norwich
Norfolk NR6 5DR, UK

www.canterburypress.co.uk

British Library Cataloguing in Publication data
A catalogue copy of this book is available
from the British Library

978 1 84825 791 7

Typeset by Regent Typesetting
Printed and bound in Great Britain by
CPI Group (UK) Ltd, Croydon

Contents

Preface   vii

1   The Elephant in the Room   1
2   Watching Over in Community   29
3   Faith in Oversight   50
4   Multi-Congregation Leadership   74
5   Watching Over with Integrity   105
6   A New Calling   133

Bibliography   151
Index of Names and Subjects   163

Preface

If you want to know what is happening in the life of our churches today then look at the changes taking place locally in our congregations. The ways in which they are being supported, reorganized and encouraged to grow are changing, but in many places this change is neither recognized nor understood. Denominational life with its weight of meetings, synods and committees continues as if nothing has happened. The time has come to talk more openly about a challenging and quite different situation. I hope this book will encourage more debate and public discussion.

There are many supportive ideas being offered to understand the changing nature of ministry and mission in the local church, but these are fragmentary and address only some of the most important changes. The main change to be understood is the way in which many congregations are being grouped together. In some large part this is a consequence of the reduction in the number of full-time clergy. The combined effect is to challenge accepted practices and understandings of local ministry. There does not appear to be one coherent theological or pastoral approach which will inform and support those congregations joined together in large groupings. Similarly there seems to be little available for clergy called to ministries in such situations.

If you want to know where much of the stress, pain and hurt in many of our local churches is, listening to what members and ministers are saying will present a striking picture. Very many people of goodwill who seek to serve their local communities express a sense of being 'let down' by their denomination and unsupported in what they are attempting to achieve. Decisions which shape their ministries and affect their future are felt to be made at a distance, are inadequately explained and often defended by the use of outdated legislation and unconnected denominational practice. These damaged vocations and ministries need to be tended.

At the same time, innovative solutions which will create the future shape of the Church are being pioneered. This book is for all those people caught up in such demanding situations. The more I have consulted and listened, the more convinced I have become that a book of this kind needs to be written. It draws together accumulated wisdom and experience using theological reflection in order to be of assistance in some small way to the many in these challenging multi-congregation situations.

My deliberate emphasis on description followed by theology followed by practice provides a framework for such ministries. Not to begin in this way would be to surrender to pragmatism. The first two chapters set out the situation in our churches as I observe it. Also described are the approaches which I consider to be most appropriate and relevant. I hope that these chapters will form an accessible introduction to a complex subject and enable readers to recognize their own situations. Chapter 3 examines the theological background to this particular kind of ministry by using historical and ecumenical sources. Chapter 4 draws on some leadership theories in order to offer support to such ministries and suggests an overarching framework using the controversial method of organizational modelling. Chapter 5 develops this thinking in a way which is intended to support those called to leadership in multi-congregation situations and help them to find sustenance for themselves. I have seen many without this support who have been changed by the experience of more responsibility, and not always for the better. Chapter 6 draws together theory and practice, and structures the ideas set out in previous chapters in what I hope is an attractive and helpful way.

This book develops in some detail ideas about local ministry and about ministries of oversight which I have touched on briefly in other pieces of writing. I have also revisited some very familiar places which will be known to theological educators and to those engaged in ministerial training and formation. My continuing experience says that what is familiar to some remains foreign territory to others. Old and new ideas do sometimes connect to give deeper insights and understandings. By bringing together the familiar, the theoretical, the pragmatic and the new, it is my hope that in this one book much essential ground will be covered.

I have tried to stand alongside those in the local church and express what they see and feel. It has been important for me to link the traditions from which we come to the active life of a Church which is always in transition. Each denomination has some core non-negotiable aspects relating to its foundation and history. Some of these add to the richness of what we experience as church today; others become diminished in their significance as new ways of discovering faith and forming community become accepted as valuable and necessary. Multi-congregation ministries are here to stay, and all those called to live and work in them have to learn how to travel together towards this new stage in Christian ministry. We need to exchange experience through engaged conversation as we journey on the way.

To produce this book at all has required considerable colleagueship and a willingness to share ideas. I am grateful to my colleagues at York St John University in the Department of Education and Theology, who commented on my ideas. Colleagues of long standing have also added to my ability to reflect on the experience of local congregational ministry. Significant among these are the Revd Jane Day, the Revd Keith Elford, Canon Dr Robin Greenwood, the Revd Pam Macnaughton of CPAS, the Revd Jane Natrass, the Revd Mark Sanders and the Revd Clare Sanders. My friends and colleagues in the Church of Sweden have shared their experience of being the local church with me for more than 30 years. Particular among them are the Revd Anders Alberius, the Revd Peter Wänehag and his colleagues in the Kalmar grouping of parishes, Deaconess Anna Lundblad-Mårtensson, Bishop Lars-Göran Lönnemark and Mrs Elizabeth Lönnemark. To all I am enormously grateful. I have tried to make these ideas available across the denominations and relevant to situations across mainland Europe as well as in Britain and Ireland. The editorial guidance given by Christine Smith from Canterbury Press has made my text much easier to follow. As always, the ways in which I have developed the ideas of others alongside my own remain entirely my responsibility.

Malcolm Grundy
Ash Wednesday, 2015

I

The Elephant in the Room

This book is about mission and ministry within local church communities. It is not about regrouping congregations to manage decline but about whether God is calling us all to be the Church in new ways. It is about what it feels like to work and worship in congregations which find themselves in a new situation – joined with several or many other local congregations – with or without their willing agreement, and sharing a priest or team of clergy and other authorized ministers. It is for those clergy who are asked or required to work in different and new ways from the ones which excited and motivated their original vocation, and who find themselves with responsibility for large groupings of congregations, all of which they could not possibly see every Sunday. It is for members of teams, whether paid, house for duty, retired clergy or volunteers, who pastor, nurture and help to minister in these changing contexts. This book is also for church leaders, formed in old ways of achieving congregational growth and development and now in senior or supervisory roles, who find themselves responsible for reshaping the life of local churches.

This first chapter is called 'The Elephant in the Room' because a largely unnamed and unexamined situation already faces the historic denominations. We are wrestling with the challenges of reshaping and sustaining effective local ministry in newly regrouped situations. In 2011, 71 per cent of the Church of England's parishes were in multi-congregation amalgamations of one kind or another. There is much wisdom to draw on from the secular world about mergers or joining organizations in a new relationship. Part of this wisdom says that the reason many mergers fail to reach their intended outcomes is that insufficient account is taken of the differing cultures in the groups which are being partnered. Without an understanding of the many different stories and histories which are being brought together it is enormously difficult to create a new identity which embraces all those who are involved.

The issues which arise in the reorganization and amalgamation of a company or charity are the same as those encountered when joining congregations of the same or different denominations. Sometimes, a new situation is hardly acknowledged at all and the parent organization carries on as if nothing has changed. Often, leaders and synods collude to perpetuate what a number of writers and researchers call 'family secrets'. In his book *Generation to Generation: Family Process in Church and Synagogue*, Edwin Friedman suggests that family secrets act as the 'plague in the arteries of communication; they cause stoppage in the general flow and not just at the point of their existence' (Friedman, 1985, p. 27).

What are the family secrets being kept about multi-congregation ministries? Friedman recommends establishing 'a non-anxious presence in the midst of anxious systems'. This book attempts to be just such a presence, which will enable the exploration of a situation which already exists and which can cause both panic and defensive reaction. It explores how faith can be nurtured and developed in local communities of Christians where the stability and guidance once available through a resident priest or minister can no longer be expected. The lack of ownership about how our denominations have already changed is something of a scandal. If this narrative can 'tell it as it is' then others can judge what requires further revision and what lessons learned need further expansion and denominational adaptation and ownership.

Begin with a vision

I once had a colleague who was an Irish Jesuit priest. When listening to complaints from congregation members about their various situations he would ask them in exasperation about what they hoped the local church could be like: 'Would you know it if you saw it?' he asked. The way I see what Christianity could and perhaps should look like expressed in the life of a local congregation has its origin in the time when I worked as a young industrial chaplain, developing what some would now call a pioneer ministry or a *fresh expression* of the presence of the Church in an industrial community. I was asked if I could offer some Sunday duty in a parish close to where we lived in the east end of Sheffield. My former vicar told me that the priest there had just retired and that this was a special and unusual congregation. That priest was Alan Ecclestone and he had been vicar of Darnall, a parish of 27,000 in a steelmaking and engineering area, from 1948 to 1969. Ecclestone had a reputation. Together with his wife, Delia, he was almost obsessed with how to develop and nurture a vision within the life of local congregations and their wider communities. Instead of the usual church committees and councils he established something new and quite different. There was a weekly and participative parish meeting where topics of national and international concern were discussed alongside issues within the life of the churches. Long before liturgical innovation he had established a eucharistic liturgy, around a west-facing altar surrounded by the congregation. He was an early advocate of women's ordination and a regular lecturer for the Workers' Educational Association.

Ecclestone retired to Cumbria and produced a series of books which became spiritual classics. Among these is his *Staircase for Silence*, where he took the writings of the poet, mystic and visionary Charles Péguy (1873–1914) and asked again and again what life within a Christian congregation or community should be like. Ecclestone linked spirituality and theology with human science and community development ideas. What he did not want in a local congregation was a group of people struggling to survive or concerned primarily with their own lives. The vision he wanted to share is that within whatever is done by Christian communities, and in their worship, something of the Creator God can be experienced. He writes this about the inner life of such a group of people:

The parish means a body of people drawn and held together in a spirit that prompts the members to care for, respect and love each other. It is the embodiment in any place of the I-in-You, You-in-Me relationship which Christ prayed for. Larger than the family which has its own special intimacies and responsibilities, the parish so conceived has the job of nurturing all its members that they may, in New Testament terms, grow up to their full stature in Christ. (Ecclestone, 1977, p. 76)

Ecclestone goes on to write about what he called the 'parish', which in practical terms we might call 'the congregation', in a way that asks why and how it should relate to the worlds in which the members of this congregation live and work:

Such a body would ever be seeking to do two kinds of work; the one within itself in relating its members ever more genuinely to each other, the other in shaping a common attitude towards the life of the world in which it is set. Learning to speak the truth together in love, its members would form a community not withdrawn from but actively engaged in the world, and experiencing in an ever deepening fashion a communion of transcendent character. (p. 77)

It remains the motivation for my own ministry that such communities can be established, nurtured and replicated. The challenge for us all now is to find new ways in which this fundamental Christian sense of committed community can be nurtured across changed boundaries. Drawing from this 'vision' of the congregation or parish, two things can be observed.

The first is what we might speak of as human interaction. It is almost accidental, caused by geography, proximity to an accessible and welcoming group of people or an approachable minister; but it also speaks of the nature of God and of a community attempting to model themselves on the person and teaching of Jesus Christ. It is a search for faith which is both deeply personal and can be deepened by worship and prayer alongside others. It is what many long for, and some find, if only in passing moments, in the meaningful life of a local Christian community.

4

The second thing to be observed is that such times and special moments of community are not always present, or observable, in local congregations. The ideas developed in this book, with its emphasis on multi-congregation ministries, begin with the hope that, from a rich history of worship and devotion, something of a renewed vision, a renewed calling from God, can be found. Ecclestone offers words of hope to us and other like-minded people:

> Scattered among the people in our fragmented churches today are those who hunger for something other than that they see, who are in pain because the church they belong to seems hopelessly stuck fast in a way of life that by no stretch of imagination can be described in terms of leaven, or salt or light, who realize daily that the words which are used to speak of the Church are far from being embodied in it. They know that the fellowship talked of does not take hold in a workmanlike way of the intricate fabric of human affairs nor confront the world in any decisive fashion. (p. 77)

It is this 'itch' for something other which is experienced within congregations of many different denominations. There is also the frustration of local clergy and their immediate superiors in trying to achieve any lasting workable solutions. A similar situation might be true of the one-minister congregation, but it takes on a different nature in the tasks of responsibility for several congregations.

Developing themes

It is no longer possible to go on with our local church life, with our congregations being little more than loosely related both to one another and perhaps to their denomination. We have to learn, in Ecclestone's words, how to enable a church to do the work of 'relating its members ever more genuinely to each other'.

The themes of this book are about the nature of God, about what the early Church intended to achieve when it first established a structure for the care of multi-congregational groupings, about the views of ecumenical colleagues on ministries of oversight, and what we can learn from others about how organizations work. It is an invitation to a new resolve. A priest in Sweden once said to me, 'There are no carpets in our house'; he meant that in the honesty and trust of their family life they did not 'sweep things under carpets' but chose to confront issues and one another in ways which allowed a different kind of honesty.

Ecclestone invites a pilgrim group to set out on a journey. The first step of which is to acknowledge that some fundamental changes have already taken place and that many more are needed.

Let us suppose then that such people get together, whether clergy or laity or both, for no other purpose than to try to find out what being a parish in process of renewal could mean at this present time, opening their hearts and minds to each other, making the communication between themselves and God of one piece throughout, facing the world in the most sensitive and fearless way and stringently examining their own conduct within it ... Clearly they must ask themselves how else could such a Body be formed and manifest itself in the life of the world today? (p. 78)

Changes in local ministry

Alan Ecclestone worked in a situation where he had the care of only one congregation. Using my initial vision, we now need to explore the advantages and questions which arise when congregations are joined together and have a different relationship with their clergy. A strengthening of local identity within a wider grouping of congregations can have a renewing and mission-focused effect. Set out below are some of these changed situations. They can be examined and developed as a basis for ministerial and congregational debate – and form the beginning of our practical and theological exploration.

> ## How to overcome a sense of loss

The most immediate feeling for congregation and community members when there are fewer resident clergy is a sense that one of the fundamental tenets of local church life has been lost. The image of the resident 'good shepherd' who knows and is known by the 'flock' remains strong. Something is lost when a personal one-to-one relatedness with the stipendiary minister is no longer possible. This sense of loss can also be felt outside the congregation by the wider community, and has to be acknowledged as a diminution of the place of the Church in the life of a nation.

It may be a vocational loss also for those who are ordained, many of whom experience the call to ministry as a pastoral one combined with a sacramental and preaching role. The greatest privilege of ordained ministry is to be close to a group of people and be able to share in all the ups and downs of their lives. Having to 'look after' many congregations can be a severe bereavement, since this sense of a person-to-person ministry is taken away. The weight of administration and organization can seem heavy unless this new way of being the Church in a locality becomes a shared responsibility. The vocational re-creation of the way in which a 'watching-over' relationship, understood and accepted by congregations, can be achieved becomes a primary task.

> ## How to provide adequate pastoral care

The absence of a full-time resident minister raises the immediate question of how local pastoral care can be provided within an overall concept of oversight. We are familiar with the view of certain local churchgoers that there has not been adequate pastoral care 'unless the vicar has visited'. In the majority of congregations and communities this situation has to be acknowledged to be no more. The task of the full-time minister is to devolve pastoral care and to ensure adequate training for local groups.

Pastoral care is wider than just caring for individuals. It includes responding to community needs and making corporate responses about local issues. Community groups welcome the presence of the Church, even expecting its members to attend gatherings and perhaps offer church buildings and facilities. Pastoral care is working with others to ensure that all those who are in need in a community receive adequate provision. The establishment of post offices in churches and the joint work in running food banks for those in need is often done across local boundaries and without more than the affirmation and consent of the stipendiary minister. Practical instances of 'watching over' a whole community can build new relationships and help to establish a sense of shared identity.

➢ How to delegate with trust
Working out who will do many of the jobs in the local church previously been done by a minister is a major question. It can be resolved by establishing a new working relationship with church officers and key congregation members. One stipendiary minister has responsibility for overall local oversight; many have authorized local ministries, while the majority remain, as always, as volunteers. The ways in which decisions are made, the authority to carry out decisions and the means of their evaluation become real and different issues. Underlying all of them is the need to create a new atmosphere of trust. This is tested through the experience of how delegation with trust and accountability are put into practice.

➢ How to welcome newcomers
The absence of the same minister week by week means that it becomes the real responsibility of members of the congregation to welcome newcomers. Their task is not only to welcome people before and after services but to decide on appropriate follow-up or referral. Which of the ordained or commissioned staff needs to be informed? How can approaches be made to newcomers without it being oppressive or without confidences being broken, particularly if the newcomers are part of a small community and are known to others in activity or voluntary groups? Are people attending because of a family event – a

baptism or a funeral – and what has happened to bring them back into a church building and a Christian community? Who will decide what to do if they come once or twice and are then not seen again? In a new way it will be the responsibility of those in regular attendance at one congregation who can observe and decide on this.

> **How to provide for the needs of many age groups**
The provision of support for small groupings within already small congregations has been a problem for some time. A resident minister can be alert to ways in which this can be overcome. One great advantage of multi-congregation situations, especially if made up of small congregations, is that it is possible for 'membership' groups, whether for teenagers or for adults, to be formed across the group. It is good for people to see that they are not the only ones joining a church – that they are not 'odd'. Joint initiation preparation can emphasize the concept that newcomers are joining a nationwide and international Church as well as a particular congregation. The bereaved may welcome someone from a local congregation, or if they prefer they can be visited by someone who does not know them. In affirming and necessary ways, training and support can be given within the wider grouping of congregations for such essential pastoral work.

> **How to sense direction with an absent full-time minister**
The effect of fewer locally resident ministers and larger groupings of local congregations is that the minister or priest cannot be physically present often enough to be effective as an immediate shaper of direction. Fairly balanced Sunday time in a grouping of four or five congregations means that the full-time person cannot be present at the main service more than once a month or so. In groupings of up to 20, the principal minister may be seen only every three months or at times when there is a service where all congregations join together. This situation will apply to the multiplicity of meetings and group activities which take place in the various congregations.

Agreement needs to be reached and accepted across the congregational grouping and with local church officers about when the full-time stipendiary minister will need to be present and when representative attendance at a meeting or event is delegated to someone else. In this type of situation the essential theological and practical concept which I call devolved local oversight takes on an urgent and essential relevance. Without it communication breaks down, resentment and misunderstanding grows, leading to an absence of shepherding and of trust.

> ## How to encourage liturgical and musical innovation

One major difficulty for the 'oversight group' and for the full-time minister and team is to keep the momentum for liturgical change alive. The need to oversee worship and encourage innovation is fundamental. When clergy cannot see these changes through in a systematic way problems can emerge. Every church will have its own tradition and there may be considerable local pressure to 'keep things as they are'. Yet even worship done well gets stale, and poor liturgies deteriorate rapidly. The primary objective is to offer the very best of a particular congregation's tradition.

A major and emerging question will need to be answered: who is the developer and overseer of liturgies across a group of parishes? Can and should the full-time grouping leader be 'hands on' in liturgical development in each congregation? If not, where does this primary responsibility lie? Whoever does appear, whether on Sunday or midweek, must be seen to be sharing oversight with the principal minister – and working to an agreed policy. They need to be familiar with planned developments in liturgy and act as part of the development of worship with those who are regularly present in a congregation on Sundays.

A parallel objective across a grouping of congregations is to develop and maintain a kind of worship, say over a month, which provides variety of access for different age groups and their needs. The introduction of 'Messy Church' midweek or on Sundays, or of 'Café Church', may provide new types of worship which add to rather than threaten traditional local worship patterns. Innovation and adequate liturgical provision needs to be balanced across a grouping. Each congregation puts its own character on a liturgy even if it shares a common structure with those of others. This distinctiveness should continue to be valued and its essence explained and nurtured.

> ### How to share expertise on buildings maintenance
One benefit to be gained across large groupings of congregations is that a wide range of talent and expertise may be available. The complexities of dealing with conservation agencies, architects, denominational committees and fundraising can be shared. There may be no threat to any buildings or their conservation in a grouping but there can be a great advantage in sharing experience and in not having to 'reinvent the wheel'. There is a major advantage in establishing good relationships with appropriate officers across a multi-congregation grouping.

The vexing question of financing, authorizing and supervising building maintenance is likely to remain with each local congregation and community. Most prefer this to be the case and have a strong and proprietorial sense of ownership for their local church building. The preservation and adaptation of a church building is important for local communities. Necessity and opportunity can combine to provide creative new partnership both for the wider use of buildings and for gaining a variety of sources for funding. While new partnerships may cause suspicion and ripples of mistrust, these can be overcome with careful explanation about the motives which drive the reasons for new alliances.

> ### How to communicate between congregations – and with the ministers
The most important feature of life in larger congregational units is communication. This is the primary responsibility of the full-time minister and the oversight group of ministers and

church officers for the whole area. Plans made and decisions reached need to be communicated. In an age of easy communication a weekly corporate email or revised page on a website is not beyond possibility. Communication and administration are facilitated best by an administrator who works across the whole group.

An additional advantage of multi-congregation units is that they can share in the joint financing of such an administrator, and perhaps an office in a convenient central location. Printed communication is the traditional method of communication within congregations, and newsletters, noticeboards and pew-sheets can be used to ensure that as many people as possible are aware of plans, events and proposed changes. This could easily be expanded to create a team, benefice or deanery magazine with a competent editor to enable good communication and provide another way in which those in different congregations can continue to learn about one another.

➤ **How to remain outward-facing**
One immediate danger which can arise from the absence of ministerial direction is that a congregation looks in on itself for security and is concerned primarily with its own needs and survival. The outward-facing nature of congregational life needs to be preserved at all times. Care for the community and a concern for those in need must be a primary activity. Relating to other congregations and community groups in a 'non-anxious' way remains essential and emphasizes the distinctive contributions which Christian communities can make.

Failure to be outward-looking may lead to congregationalism and ultimately to a sectarian attitude, set apart from community life. Active engagement with local issues and support for international relief and education agencies will renew the inner life of a congregation and help create new partnerships and alliances.

This is not an exhaustive list, but it gives a flavour of the issues raised as these changes become commonplace in the life of our local churches and denominations. The Church in which our congregations are set is also changing in important ways. These changes affect the life of local congregations in inescapable ways.

An expensive church

Significant for many long-time church members is how much it costs to be a committed member of a congregation and of a denomination. This is more than ever before. Historic resources and investments, and in northern Europe the support from a 'church tax', are diminishing at a predictable and rapid rate while costs for supporting ministry and providing pensions are rising. This raises a number of questions about expected levels of commitment to the congregation and the denomination. Such costs are less of an issue for 'new' Christians, many of whom would expect to pay a substantial amount monthly or annually for membership of a gym, golf club or professional association. The significance, or difference, with a local congregation paying a large share of its wider costs to a denomination is a changed relationship. For some, paying to a denomination ceases to be 'generous giving' in response to a generous God, and becomes a tax to be avoided whenever possible. In such a transaction the relationship becomes changed. From being a community, or communion, where identity and belonging are represented in its title and through its officers, the relationship becomes one of resentment and distrust regarding money taken and spent by a denomination, even to pay and house its clergy.

The consequence of a congregation which meets the cost of its clergy and staff is that those who 'pay the piper' want to 'call the tune'. Local church officers and their congregations want a significant say in the choice of minister and may resent external imposition (felt, if not actual) in the choice of a new minister. They may feel that since they are paying for a minister some sense of direction might be given about what he or she does with their time and the emphases they give in their ministry. Particularly in multi-congregation situations, members may get the impression that they are paying more into the funds of a denomination than they are getting back in ministerial coverage. As one Yorkshire Dales person commented when I was trying to explain our parish share system, 'What you mean, Archdeacon, is that you want us to pay more for less!' While it has never been a principle of many denominations that 'you pay for what you get', contributing to a common fund to support churches in challenging social situations can be resented. In a variation on this general theme, in some dioceses and denominations the congregation, or group of congregations, are expected to pay the full cost of ministry. Again, while there are merits in this especially in terms of local responsibility, the downside is that only the 'strongest' churches survive, those with oversight of wider, less robust or viable groupings find deployment of ministers and strategic reorganization of congregations harder to achieve.

Money, and where the power lies for decisions about how it is spent, can contribute to a lack of realism about what kind of change is viable and the 'family secrets' being perpetuated. At the same time finance is driving change in ways I have described. A strong notion of propriety from a local congregation may restrict the sense of membership of a wider ecclesial community. Equally, a strong sense of local ownership can breed resistance to amalgamation and grouping within the local area of a denomination. Wanting to 'get what you pay for' can run counter to a sense of mutuality inherent in the relationship, expected but not always well expressed, between a local congregation and the wider Church to which, in whatever denominational way, it belongs.

In this one single altered transaction a relationship becomes changed. While membership of a denomination is acknowledged, to many it means little. People who are new to faith or who have moved from one denomination to another find that structures of their new denomination often go unexplained, particularly with regard to the life of a local congregation. If any reorganization is proposed and a ministerial relationship is changed then the whole question of the nature of 'belonging' to a denomination can be called into question. Change can be and often is threatening. When the relationships of power and trust become disturbed, and if insensitive external intervention appears to be the cause of the change, then the path to 'grow' into something new becomes even more painful and difficult.

Money can be a difficult topic to discuss within the life of a church. The balance between faith and practicality is always a sensitive one. The need to raise new funds or to economize should not be the primary cause or reason for change, but unless this first fundamental relational difference is named it will not be possible to move to the acceptance of new and perhaps more effective patterns of life for local churches. Generous financial giving also represents a commitment to faith.

An inclusive Church

The changing nature and calling within ordained ministry represents a fundamental change in the life of a local church which has yet to be completely accepted in a meaningful way. In most denominations women and men work in an equal way and most ministerial appointments are available to both. The Church of England, as part of an international family of episcopal churches, has only just moved to the opening up of the episcopate to women, some 20 or more years after accepting women as priests. The Methodist, Baptist and Free Churches, with the Salvation Army, have equal ministerial status, some since their inception.

The consequence of this for today's church, to a greater extent than ever before, is that women are in positions of ministerial leadership, often leading staff groupings of both men and women. Congregations have responded in various ways to these changes, and women themselves need further opportunities to demonstrate alternative interpretations of oversight. Many aspects of resistance to men and women being eligible for vacancies are covert, hardly acknowledged and not well expressed. There remain congregations who will not accept a woman as their minister.

Some congregations retain practices which relate to the norms and procedures of a previous age, preferring liturgies designed by past generations and music to reflect such an approach to congregational life. These are sometimes known as 'islands of isolation and reversion'. Many congregations, singly or in groupings, wrestle with other issues of inclusiveness. Some find it difficult to dialogue with those of other faiths while others are still coming to terms with the local demands of ecumenical relationship. How national churches decide to address international and worldwide cultural questions of sexuality in relation to marriage and to family life will also affect the decisions which local clergy and congregations will be required to make.

An engaged laity

As with the increasingly significant place of ordained women in the ministry of churches at many levels, so also the increasing significance of authorized lay ministries and voluntary lay ministries brings a large number of new players to the church door. Significant also is the engagement of laypeople in the active life of their local church. This is quite a different age from the one where bishops in episcopal churches could redistribute their clergy without the threat of challenge, or even when private patrons could suggest clergy to the bishop for appointments. Consultation is expected, and the right of veto for appointments is an assumption if not always a reality.

In many congregations, in the past predominantly in the countryside but now commonplace also in urban areas, it is a group of laypeople, with the churchwardens or other appointed 'stewards', who are responsible for local ministry. The building has to be maintained, local funds raised, social and community events organized and non-eucharistic worship overseen. In a number of these places a new sense of joy is being experienced. All-age worship services, whether on Sunday or midweek, bring in many newcomers, and some of these choose to get more committed and share in what often feels like a worthwhile local community enterprise. This can be both a relief and a credit to the stipendiary minister and those who 'oversee' the larger group of congregations. While good and trusting relationships can enable such energized growth to take place, there is also responsibility on the ordained to share the 'ethos' of the denomination and to ensure that legal safeguards are in place and that those with denominational authority to conduct worship have an active involvement.

There are many ways of holding the responsibility for oversight and ways in which congregations can share in ministry and celebrate membership of the wider grouping. It is the framework of these 'many ways' which I shall be exploring in later chapters. In multi-congregation ministries the authorized full-time stipendiary minister is expected to work with and alongside a wide variety of colleagues, each with a particular responsibility for ministry of one kind of another. The senior or full-time stipendiary minister will find themselves exercising local oversight.

A description of these situations brings an awareness of the most significant change in the local life of congregations. It is an impetus which is natural to 'new Christians' but one which has had to be relearned by many others. Mission is a loaded concept and one which has developed in significance in the priorities of local and national church leaders.

A mission-minded Church

We live in denominations where much activity is shaped by the desire for mission. It is important now to undertake a reassessment of what is generally meant by mission. It is apparent in any understanding of local or national life in our churches today that the emphasis on mission has become paramount. Many of the new church ordinals describe one of the main elements of the work of a bishop as a 'leader in mission'. This same new emphasis works its way down to a similar requirement in the work of a local minister and the purpose of mission activities in the development of congregational life. This stems out even further in the attitude towards continuing to invest heavily in the work of church schools by the Roman Catholic Church and the Church of England, and in the new opportunities offered by the educational policy of successive UK governments enabling 'faith schools' to be established by wealthy individuals and groups who form trusts and charities for this explicit purpose.

Mission as the working out of faith-sharing with interested individuals or groups can take many forms. We know that in the New Testament accounts of his ministry, Jesus gave emphasis both to 'making all people my disciples' and to recognizing the 'signs of the kingdom' in everyday human activity. Perhaps the most interesting and relevant place to begin to examine how the Church understands these two aspects of its mission is the debate the mission agencies had to have regarding the change in their work; from a situation where European nations had 'empires' with colonies and national territories around the world to a new 'post-colonial' world. There was once a well-used phrase: 'Trade follows the flag and the Bible follows trade.' But once the age of empire ended and the integrity of other faiths came to be recognized and understood, this kind of 'proselytizing' missionary endeavour had to be re-evaluated.

In the early 1950s this new situation was recognized as the World Council of Churches set up a project to explore the nature of mission in the modern world and in particular what it called 'the missionary structure of a congregation'. It is important at this stage to note that the emphases were not initially on the need to draw more people into the life of local congregations but to improve the quality of congregational life so that committed members might be a more effective presence in their chosen sphere of work or activity.

This change of attitude is reflected in the journal *International Review of Mission*. In an article published in 1965, Michael Jackson wrote about mission in England. Speaking particularly about industrial missions across Europe, he described mission in a different way. Beginning with the establishing of 'diplomatic missions' in overseas countries by nation states, he argues from the premise of establishing a Christian presence. This opening position for the UK and much of mainland Europe stems from a feeling that the churches had become separated from the everyday life and work of those engaged in industry and commerce. What was needed in terms of mission was not what they called 'church extension' but an engagement from the inside with the concerns of everyday life. Jackson wrote:

> If no-one takes the world of industry seriously there is no industrial mission and no industrial mission projects; or, if there were such a project, it would be a self-regarding religious institution, using industry for other purposes – as a place for pastoral visiting, for instance, or for capturing prisoners for church parade. (Jackson, 1965, p. 158)

Maddy Thung, who was one of the principal participants in the WCC project, describes a future Church as they saw it as one which 'reformulates evangelism and mission as a Christian way of living rather than as a propagandistic recruitment of members' (Thung, 1976, p. 68). This thinking led churches and congregations into increased social engagement and the establishment of a network of 'laity centres' across Europe aimed at equipping lay people to contribute in an informed way to the social and political issues of their day.

A vast body of literature has developed over the past 30 years which encourages parishes and clergy to move their emphasis from being pastorally and community minded to becoming focused on mission to individuals. One person who has encouraged learning from the missionary methods of developing countries, and the man who first coined the phrase 'emerging church', is Eddie Gibbs. The Emerging Church movement includes both mission-focused groups within traditional denominations, and independent and radically different expressions of the Church. Gibbs first described this mission impetus in *I Believe in Church Growth* (1981), and he has continued to teach and write first in the UK and then in the USA. His *Emerging Churches: Creating Christian Communities in Postmodern Cultures*, co-written with Ryan Bolger, expresses the full range of his analysis (2005).

In the UK, emphasis on evangelism and its supporting literature was given particular prominence during the Decade of Evangelism, initiated by Archbishop George Carey and put into effect by Resolution 43 of the 1988 Lambeth Conference. The principal exponents and writers in the UK were John Finney and Robert Warren. Finney published *Finding Faith Today* in 1992, which was a survey of 500 people who had come to faith between March 1990 and March 1991. Its findings were developed by Finney, then the national officer for the Decade of Evangelism, into a series of evidence-based propositions about growth. These ideas, and those of Gibbs and others, were applied by Robert Warren to attitudes from congregations about evangelism. In 1995 he succeeded Finney and published a review of progress, *Signs of Life: How Goes the Decade of Evangelism?*, at the halfway stage in 1996. At the same time he wrote *Building Missionary Congregations* which described the transition to a pastoral emphasis on mission in styles of ministry (Warren, 1995, 1996). Both books are brief in length but continue to have a wide influence on parish clergy. This whole movement has been critiqued in a most rigorous way by the theologian and educationalist John Hull in his *Mission-Shaped Church: A Theological Response* (Hull, 2006). Hull follows Jackson in pleading for mission to relate to the issues facing the presence of the Church in the world rather than an overemphasis on what he regarded as the creation of inward-looking congregations.

The Church Growth Research Programme of the Church of England is the place where statistics are gathered about amalgamations of parishes and what within them contributes to growth or decline. A report setting out the evidence called *From Anecdote to Evidence: Findings from the Church Growth Research Programme 2011–2013* sets out the situation in accessible detail (www.churchgrowthresearch.org.uk).

Evangelistic initiatives have included new forms of local ministry, with the appointment of 'pioneer ministers' introducing a non-parochial element to the work of the local church and bringing different kinds of minister into local teams. It is these Fresh Expressions encouraged in many dioceses which run counter to a 'mechanistic', ordered and controlled Church. This, running in parallel with the virtual abandonment of the extremely rigid and formal team ministries, signifies a movement towards a much less ordered and 'controlled' Church of England.

There is a pressing need to bring into the open already changed situations in the life of the local church and to analyse how these reflect and contribute to emerging understandings of life in local communities. Such an exploration reveals and emphasizes the need to establish a variety of ways of sharing faith and building up the life of local congregations without succumbing to the ever-present danger of lapsing into sectarianism and a life existing over against the world rather than fully a part of it. In already reconfigured local congregations these issues present significant challenges of a theological as well as organizational kind.

An institutionalized Church

Any layperson who generously gives their time or anyone involved in the work of their denomination as an official or senior minister will know that the current organizational ethos of their denomination consumes much of the time and resources available. It is reasonable to say that these could be better used. Important for this discussion about the nature of the Church is Gareth Morgan's analysis of the ways in which churches have come to operate. He thinks that there are parallels between the mechanization of industry and the development of bureaucratic forms of organization. Churches throughout the twentieth century have followed this pattern, becoming hamstrung by committee, and in the twenty-first century by performance indicators for its ordained and licensed ministers (Morgan, 1997, 2006).

Leaders of the contemporary Church, while often frustrated in their attempts, have to hold a balance between seeing a historic stable institution with leaders who have set roles and inherited functions and an organization with the contemporary characteristics of aims and objectives, mission statements and even 'measurable outcomes' in the way that a commercial or public service organization would assess its successes and failures. There is a great danger in seeing churches as 'special' or different types of community which cannot, because of their supposed difference, be subjected to the same kind of analysis as any other grouping of people who combine to achieve specific purposes.

Questions need to be asked about the life and work of a congregation or a denomination at a regional or national level where so many seem to be frustrated by complicated and time-wasting procedures and committee structures. Bishop Stuart Cross, a former colleague, once remarked after a long and frustrating series of meetings, 'Never before in the course of human history has so little been achieved by so many in so long!', referring to Churchill's famous wartime speech. Those who study the nature of national churches and denominations become drawn into an important discussion: in what ways are they institutions and in what ways are they organizations? Committees and interference from outside bodies can frustrate and confuse local church members. Complicated systems allow those who disagree with a policy, or who want their point of view to dominate, the opportunity to 'block' the progress of policies and ideas.

A much analysed Church

We are fortunate that sociologists and organizational thinkers have taken an interest in the place and the structure of churches in Western society. David Martin sets out 17 differing ways in which religion has a place in European societies, reflecting history, migration, persecution and revivalism (Martin, 1978, pp. 140–2). In an earlier study, used as a means of determining mission strategies using religious sociology, Fernard Boulard made a significant study of the impact of industrialization in churchgoing in northern France (Boulard, 1960). Both sociologists and theologians have commented on how the shapes of church structure and bureaucracy mirror those of industrial society.

While not addressing ecclesiastical issues directly, the academic and research theologian Simon Western attempts to analyse emerging understandings of leadership and the cultural trends which have formed them. Interestingly for this exploration, he goes on to examine and suggest the 'spaces' where leadership can flourish. This connects with my earlier observation that there is a need to create 'non-anxious' places where growth of a different kind can take place. He makes an interesting observation about the 'spirit' which a leader encapsulates and represents, which can enable re-formation.

> Leadership spirit, like leadership itself, is collective as well as personal. Leadership teams and distributed leaders have to find their communal spirit, to work well together, to embrace what is important. Much of my work as a consultant is to get groups and individuals to pause, to hesitate to create a space just for cognitive thinking or reflecting on a challenge, but also to re-engage as humans on a journey, to reconnect with each other, to share stories and rediscover mythos and their leadership spirit. (Western, 2008, p. 263)

Western develops what he calls 'post-heroic leadership' in reaction to the temptations to hubris commonly observed in power-gathering, hierarchy-climbing leadership. He commends the leader who 'blends extreme personal humility with intense personal will' (p. 46).

A disaffected Church

The kind of changes described so far have the consequence of creating a separation of the central from the local which, coupled with the bureaucratic busyness of leaders, has created among local congregations and clergy a sense of disaffection with the life and structures of dioceses and national churches. While wanting to be pastoral or prophetic or 'leaders in mission', many are actually totally occupied with immediate issues and are only seen by members of local congregations when there is a crisis or when difficult decisions have to be made. Too much of their time is taken up with the busyness of the present.

Writing from an international perspective, Maddy Thung, who has worked with the World Council of Churches, suggests in *The Precarious Organization: Sociological Explorations of the Church's Mission and Structure* that a national or international Church is more a social system than an institution or organization, and says it is 'recalcitrant', having characteristics which are obstinately defiant of authority (Thung, 1976). She says that national churches and international denominations are difficult to oversee, since on the one hand they have ultimate goals about the transformation of society and on the other they have members who seek to achieve those goals using different and often contradictory ends. An initial reaction might suggest that it is impossible to arrive at an agreed description and analysis even for local groupings of congregations. They are, as Thung describes, 'recalcitrant' organizations made up of disparate and often competing groups unwilling to accept what they see as external direction (p. 286).

The analogy of 'herding cats' to describe the problem of understanding, managing and leading the Church has been used by Martyn Percy. In a chapter entitled 'Herding Cats: Leadership in the Church of England' in *Anglicanism: Confidence, Commitment and Communion*, he says:

> Should it not be apparent that the organization is *not* shaped for easily defined aims, objectives and goals? Indeed, is it not obvious that the Church of England is, in a profound sense, a community of practice, bound together more by manners, habits and outlooks than it is by doctrinal agreement? Indeed, one could argue that Anglicanism, at its best, is a community of civilized disagreement? (Percy, 2013, p. 138)

The challenge is to discover the ways in which a national Church such as the Church of England can move beyond being tolerant if benign 'communities of practice', recalcitrant organizations comprising people and groups more skilled at blocking progress than in facilitating change and development towards becoming something more positive. Can its adherents become committed to 'watching over one another in community' rather than continuing to be characterized as 'a community of civilized disagreement'.

At the end of such a catalogue of changes taking place in our churches, we may be inclined to be overcome with pessimism. Instead of a doom-laden conclusion it may be possible to establish a bridge where new examples of best practice can be reflected on and shared. The creation of this kind of exchange suggests that when things go well, an enormous sense of optimism can be experienced and energy released. This need not only happen by accident, but can be created by careful analysis of what happens when new ideas and new relationships have a positive outcome. There is a fund of expertise ready to be tapped. It may come from the training and experience of laypeople in their everyday work, or from those who have reflected long on how organizations and institutions 'work' – and how they might work in more effective ways.

A learning Church

From traditional patterns of practice in the local church, new relationships and new configurations mean that learning can be done in a new way. Various theories and strands of theology need to be explored before the potential within multi-congregation groupings can be realized. In his book *The Fifth Discipline*, Peter Senge proposes that what distinguishes learning organizations from other types is the display of certain basic 'dimensions' or 'component technologies'. He identifies five of these, which when they converge give the characteristics for those engaged in the team, group or organization that essential 'buzz' (Senge, 1990, pp. 6–14).

Senge's five 'disciplines' are: personal mastery, mental models, building a shared vision, team learning, and systems thinking. The most important of these characteristics is his 'fifth discipline', systems thinking. He says that this one discipline integrates all the others; it is the most important because a key problem with much that is written about management and leadership is that rather simplistic frameworks are applied to complex systems.

Although Senge calls his fifth discipline, with some enthusiasm, systems thinking, this might be contested as lacking in its purest outworking as an academic theory. What he describes is the 'energy' generated when a number of factors come into play between a group of people or 'group of groups' in an organization. Senge has acted as a thought leader describing what he calls a 'learning organization'. His comments relate directly to the energy created when ecclesiastical colleagueship stimulates:

> When you ask people what it is like being part of a great team, what is most striking is the meaningfulness of the experience. People talk about being part of something larger than themselves, of being connected, of being generative. It became quite clear that, for many, their experience as part of truly great teams stand out as singular periods of life lived to the fullest. Some spend the rest of their lives trying to recapture that spirit. (p. 13)

It is the four disciplines leading to the fifth which enables a framework for my analysis and further development.

A new starting point

As this examination of multi-congregation ministry develops it will be possible to explore a fundamental question: Whether and how a concept used by the first Christian communities to meet a need when working together can be experienced in a new way. The need was for how those with responsibility could 'watch over' groupings of local Christian communities. The word used for this was *episkope* – a word with rich meaning but one which became restricted to describing the work of bishops. We know that from the earliest days of Christianity the Jerusalem congregation attempted, possibly mirroring the Essenes, a form of 'holding all things in common' (Acts 4.32–35) and that reciprocal care with collections for the less well off was fundamental to the life of its communities. Internal cohesion and shared values were possible for a small and growing organization with its particular sense of ownership and continuity. These communities were soon to face internal and external challenges so it was essential that a shared sense of identity of faith and practice was established. Social and cultural developments would affect the life and leadership of these communities. After Christianity became a civic religion, with its leaders appointed by the rulers of nation-states, this sense of a mutual and internally governed community of congregations was diminished.

There is now the need to suggest a new definition which draws on the richness of a concept and explores just what was and is needed in the oversight of local congregations. It could be described as 'watching over one another in community'. Such an exploration of the potential of *episkope* or 'watching over' can move a discussion about the changed structure of churches and congregations on to a new place. A former chief rabbi of the United Hebrew Congregations of the Commonwealth, Jonathan Sacks, wrote in *The Times* of 18 August 2012 that an understanding is needed which 'breaks away from the hierarchical relationship of leaders and followers and builds on the Hebrew concept of collective responsibility'.

An expanded definition is explored by David Cornick with reference to the Lambeth Quadrilateral in *Unity in Process: Reflections on Ecumenism* (Barrett, 2012, p. 61). He says that this discussion is not only about the changing life of the local church but also about how we are to redefine our understanding of our denominations and the relationship of local churches to a 'parent body'. He asks questions about how we care for one another, respect differences and reshape community in ways which twenty-first-century pilgrims will follow.

Reciprocal care and respect in multi-congregation settings makes me want to ask about the fundamental understanding of relationships within our denominations. Should relationships mirror structures, and firmly defined roles separate colleagues trying to develop a common vision with a loyalty to the same denomination? Are our denominations (and do they have to be) centralized with an increasing tendency towards control or are they, in practice and general understanding, a community of congregations which draw on a range of identities to give them meaning? Roles have to be observed and boundaries kept, but there is a bigger task. Can we follow the hare set running by Sacks and establish through trusting and developing relationships a Church with its local communities which 'breaks away from the hierarchical relationship of leaders and followers and builds on the Hebrew concept of collective responsibility'?

The relationship between leaders and congregations, clergy and parishioners in a largely 'voluntary' organization requires revisiting. Martyn Percy puts it like this:

> Those charged with the ministry of oversight may need to come to some understanding of how those under them learn. Often, this is done not through the simple or mechanistic transferral of principles, rules and propositions. It is, rather, through a deeper formational wisdom rooted in tactical suavity, emotional intelligence, reflexivity and responsiveness. (Percy, 2013, p. 15)

It is vitally important to explore and test out how this concept can be understood and developed locally within multi-congregation situations in new and creative ways. In what ways can ministries of oversight be legitimated and where can the advantages of collaboration be described and observed? Is it possible to identify where communities with characteristics of best practice are emerging and where an obligation to 'watch over one another in community' becomes an overriding theological and ministerial obligation? How can it become possible for groupings of congregations in a very local way to be learning communities? In important and new ways, how can those who are called to ordained and licensed lay ministries discover, or rediscover, a developing sense of vocation?

2

Watching Over in Community

What is it like to be part of an already different Church? What is it like for ministers and congregations to feel called to be the local church in a range of new ways? A vocational question, which needs to be addressed again and again, concerns the nature, shape and character that God is calling the present and future Church to become. From perceptions of this arises the important question of what kind of clergy will be needed in a Church with different shapes and new ministerial tasks and roles. There are a number of ways in which such questions can be answered, and different answers will be given by members of the same or partner congregations. Differences in the shapes of liturgy, in mission and ministry, in being 'evangelical' or 'catholic' or 'traditional', or in approaches by ministers within the same grouping will be familiar to many. These all add to a richness of interpretation and debate.

It is important to draw on the wisdom of the secular world in trying to understand what is happening in our churches, even if we accept that the Church is not 'a business' and cannot be analysed in exactly the same way. Keith Elford is a former consultant with Telos Partners, and an Anglican priest (www.elfordconsulting.co.uk). In his *Creating the Future of the Church* he has developed a simple structure which helps to explain the role of oversight in accompanying mergers and organizational change (Elford, 2013). There are three things which have to be worked at in the life of every organization, congregation or grouping of congregations, as they attempt to find new ways of working together. These are: to manage the present, to nurture identity, and to create the future (Figure 1). It is not appropriate to change another person's or organization's model but in church situations it is important to 'know the memory of the past'. For Elford, identity is 'the voice of the past'. In a conversation with him he remarked, 'our identity is what our past has made us'. It leads to a place where questions have to be explored about why a church was formed in a particular way in the first place and why it has developed in the ways that we can now observe and describe.

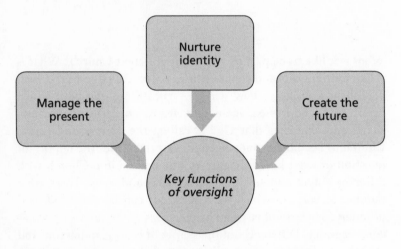

Figure 1 Key functions for the congregation and its ministers

Elford attributes and explains the origins of his work in this way:

> The model that underpins everything that follows ... does not come from the business world but was developed by a management scientist named Stafford Beer, who was a leading figure in the science of describing organizations as complex systems, and a remarkable, visionary man. St Paul likens the Church to a body with Christ as the head. Stafford Beer began by examining how fundamental organizational systems such as the human body adapt to their environment and maintain themselves successfully. His thinking is based on an enquiry into what organizations *of all kinds* do to remain viable and identifies key shared functions and characteristics. (Elford, 2013, p. 21)

While developing the ideas of Elford and basing the next sections on the characteristics identified by Stafford Beer, it is attractive to attempt to apply the analysis to the particular situation of multi-congregation ministries. How are they adapting to a changed environment, managing the present, nurturing identity and creating the future? It is in these amalgamations that churches are experiencing the greatest amount of change and where significant readaptation and vocational development are required.

Manage the present

One of the most intriguing discussions which take place about congregational life concerns the strength of memory. When congregations are brought into a new relationship with one another, past grievances, fights, hurts and memories of damage can be brought to the surface. Insecurity is a major part of this. Whenever change is proposed which disturbs traditions and power bases then defence mechanisms come into play. It is common to hear stories of village rivalries which go back centuries. It appears to be of no account that those living in the village now have no direct connection with these feuds. Other reasons suggested for the strength of memory include the relative stability of a local church population. Some do retain memories of disputes through the generations, while many will have experienced differences with clergy as they have come and then gone. The build-up of such memories is very real and has to be not only acknowledged but heard and understood as a part of the character of that local community. Understanding does not imply collusion, but does require a sensitive ear and the ability to find ways of enabling the story of one community and congregation to be heard by another.

Urban and suburban congregations present some of the same characteristics within the retention of memory as those held by rural churches, but they may have distinctive ones of their own. When being merged or associated with other congregations their memory may well be more recent and more easily and credibly articulated. The Victorian church building was generally constructed for a purpose, perhaps in response to an expanding population and housing needs, and funded by a patron of some kind. Such patronage is frequently associated with a distinctive churchmanship, whether 'high' or 'low'. Often the architecture of a building reflects this, as does the furniture, statuary and memorial tablets. Many have fine examples of stained glass in memory of an influential person or family. Almost all have memorials to remember the sacrifice of local people in a series of European and World Wars.

The more modern urban church will present a different series of memories which need to be heard and respected. These may concern the establishment or the enlargement of the building. Within living memory funds will have been raised to create a new church and to furnish it. Knowledge of the dedication of furnishings in memory of loved ones will influence attitudes to any reordering of the space and to sharing worship which requires the removal of furnishings or their relegation to a less significant place. Urban memories may also have within them mergers of other churches and congregations where small numbers or deteriorating buildings have forced closure or amalgamation. As a reminder, lists of previous and now amalgamated congregations are sometimes given to newly arrived ministers. When asked on occasion, some congregation members will still say, even after many years, that they are really members of a church which may have been closed for a very long time! Memory and its strength have to be taken very seriously when multi-congregation ministries are being created or revised.

The most significant and immediate memory which has to be understood is the story of how any group of local churches came to be formed. A tremendous amount of work is needed to accompany congregations as they come to terms with a new situation. Two factors are prominent: one is how the amalgamation was conducted by the diocese or denomination, the other is the series of local and individual situations which have been undermined by this radical change. The history of our congregations is that they are a group of people in a relationship with their community and their building who have had leadership, pastoral care and liturgical and preaching ministries from an ordained, locally based person. They have expected something of the 'good shepherd' relationship where the people knew and trusted their pastor and were known by their names. There is an element of fantasy in this 'pastoral' ideal but this model is the one which is most under threat by large groupings of congregations. The approach of a diocese or denomination towards congregational reorganization is a key part of the process of change and a major component in the forming of a memory about what has been done. The concept of scapegoat comes into play here. Someone may have to be blamed for the loss of a former kind of security, however illusory or ineffective it has been. The denomination and its officers are in the firing line. Projection of blame in this way is convenient. It can seem to absolve local congregations and their officers from responsibility for an unwelcome change. The dynamics of the negotiation of local congregational reorganization are a study in themselves and immensely relevant to this book.

There is no doubt that the process of forming agreement about where groupings for multi-congregation ministries should be made is the foundation for success or for failure and resentment. Done well, with good communication and appropriate specialist officer support, many positive aspects of a wider grouping can be envisaged. Done poorly, with little local consultation and poor communication, a vehicle for resentment can be created which can form a festering part of memory for years to come.

It is an interesting theological reflection that the strength of memory in a congregation, and even in a denomination, may be part of the reason for its establishment in the first place. Members whose origins lie in another denomination need to know why certain theological and liturgical emphases in this tradition are important. It has been suggested that the strong reference to the past when change is proposed has been learned through the 'shape' of the liturgies. Bible readings and sermons together, with the particular emphasis in the Eucharist to 'do this in remembrance of me', encourage the past to be the primary reference point for Christians or congregations considering change of any kind. None of this prevents change, but may inform initial responses to proposals. The memory of the past can also be a means of remembering experiences of renewal and resurrection which have enabled individuals and communities to move forward.

Pictures of the present

The history and methods of narrative for the formation of memory form an essential part of the management of the present. Multi-congregational situations come in very many shapes and forms, and none is exactly the same as another. Some basic configurations can be described, however. The Methodist Church has a Circuit system, where congregations have an independent life but share ministers, one of which is the Superintendent. This is the word chosen by John Wesley when he translated *episkope*. What is emerging is not a version of the Circuit System, but a range of developments which have a newness and vitality of their own.

There are three traditional, familiar arrangements of multi-congregation situations in the Church of England and it is appropriate to begin with these. First, and most formal, is the Team Ministry, second is the Group Ministry, and third are groupings of two, three or four relatively small congregations around one stipendiary minister.

Amalgamations of parishes and team ministries within the Church of England in 2011 made up 8,400 of its 12,500 parishes. Team ministries had their heyday when the prevailing atmosphere was to group parishes and congregations, often in one united benefice, with clergy in a kind of hierarchy. A team rector appointed for a stated number of years is the senior clergyperson. He or she works with a number of team vicars who may have local congregational responsibilities or specialist work across the benefice. There is often a ministry team, with readers and others 'governed' or overseen by a team council made up of representatives elected by the congregations. The diocese will have agreed a constitution for the team ministry and this gives boundaries for governance, the management of finances and the structuring of ministerial life

34

within the constituent parishes. Experience has shown that these ministries can be over-restrictive in their legalities, too structured, and highly dependent on the personalities and the 'chemistry', for better or worse, between the staff.

Group ministries are more like a collaborative partnership of equals. The clergy may well be independent and in the Church of England still hold a freehold 'living'. Cooperation across parish boundaries is optional and much depends on goodwill, a shared sense of mission and service to the community, and local ownership of the concept of voluntarily giving up a measure of independence in order that support of specialist kinds – ministries to children, teenagers and young adults, baptism visiting and bereavement support – can be offered in ways not possible for small and independent congregations. Group ministries can seem quite fragile, not sufficiently demanding of commitment, providing opportunities for local groups to 'opt out' if they wish. Groups, as with team ministries, can be clerically dominated.

What is distinctive in both these situations is a gradually developing willingness by laypeople across congregations and parish boundaries to work together. Equally distinctive is the concept of a group of clergy, usually of the same denomination but not always, working together either formally as a 'team' or by consent as a 'group'. The idea of clergy being able to work together and support one another was often thought to be a difficult one to put into practice, but in particular situations it was seen to work well. In their day, both team and group ministries were accepted as major 'new shapes' for the Church.

Of greater vintage is the grouping of up to four parishes with one stipendiary priest. Most of these groupings were originally in rural areas. These types of amalgamation are more or less manageable with one principal service-taker on Sundays, and they allow the minister to get around the parishes and local communities where they can know and be known by their congregations. The pastoral work is also just possible, and each congregation can continue to 'pretend' that they have their own vicar – even if they resent the fact that the vicarage or clergy house is in another parish!

In mapping situations which are recognizable to many, the 'history' of the creation of multi-congregation ministries can be traced. In each there are multi-layered understandings of how such arrangements have been created and how local people have responded to them. In the 'new' Church of today an even greater change has taken place. Adaptations of old parochial and ministerial models no longer work in some situations. Where one stipendiary minister has 'charge' or, as I would want to say, 'oversight' of between four and 20 congregations in nearly as many parishes, something new is needed. The changes which have already taken place are producing many examples of good practice and experiment. Many of these are pragmatic and can only be made more robust and enduring when connected to the theological and organizational understandings of the mature Church.

Describing the elephant

The large grouping of congregations constitutes a completely new situation, and presents a whole range of different pastoral, liturgical and organizational questions for the various denominations. In the Church of England this situation was foreseen in 1983 in a report by John Tiller, then Secretary of its Board of Ministry, called *A Strategy for the Church's Ministry*. Perversely, the word 'strategy' is still mistrusted by some senior leaders because of its military and secular connotations, while others worry that it gives no room for the movement of the 'Holy Spirit'. Tiller says that ultimately the deanery will become the most logical grouping for local congregations, with clergy and laity working in specialist teams (1983, p. 137). Like very many reports prepared by church committees and far-seeing individuals it was set aside at the time as being too radical. Hindsight has shown how prophetic many of these have been and we can now see the extent to which, with gradual adaptations, many of these proposals have been put into place.

Nine multi-congregation situations

From a development of one of Elford's key functions, 'managing the present', it is possible to map out and summarize some of the multi-congregation situations which will give energy to this exploration. In the following chapters theological, ecumenical and organizational analyses are set out. Only after that can we return to our local multi-congregation situations and be able to demonstrate that work in such situations can be resourced by much more than pragmatism. The nine scenarios set out below describe various types of local situation, though none will be an exact fit.

Alongside and within my outline descriptions goes the work in schools, hospitals, hospices, chaplaincies of other kinds and specialist ministries in locally based institutions. In addition there is the work of retired clergy, lay ministers and volunteers of all kinds outside the life of congregations. These essential, mission and service activities are foundational to the outward-looking imperative for any church and contribute much to community life. Such work takes up an enormous amount of time if addressed in a proper and professional way.

1 Individual congregations who share one priest

Without doubt this is the most challenging pastoral situation. Here the traditional pattern of clerical ministry is stretched to breaking point and beyond. Oversight is achieved by a multitude of appearances in random and unstructured activity. 'The Vicar' is expected to know what is happening, appear at the bedside of a sick member of the congregation and to know everyone's needs through a mixture of telepathy and osmosis.

Such situations are still common and are addressed in different ways. Most important is that the officers of a congregation discuss and agree with the sole minister on the events and meetings where attendance is essential, where it is desirable and where it need not be expected. Communication about how these priorities have been agreed is fundamental.

Pastoral care can be offered to those in crisis situations; as ever, it is expected to be given by an authorized minister. Much other pastoral care is available on an informal basis from congregation members, with their local knowledge. Communal oversight comes to the fore in such situations, but in an unstructured and informal way.

Liturgical innovation is never easy, and requires informed awareness of changes initiated by the national Church and the developing tradition of a denomination. A sense of shared local worship across congregations is already widely demonstrated through the production of common service booklets reflecting the seasons of the church year. The level of musical participation will still come at the initiative of the minister, together with local organists and musicians. A fifth Sunday in the month may give an opportunity for shared worship. All innovation will mean a painstaking and slow process which requires diplomacy and trust coupled with a sense that guided progress and movement is necessary. The great advantage in this way of working is that local cooperation has little choice but to develop through both formal and informal lines of communication.

2 *One priest with a ministry team who cover all congregations*

'Sole charge' responsibility remains a common situation. Here the responsibility for oversight, liturgical innovation, pastoral care and evangelism is shared by the ministry team. The formation of such teams, and the discussion about whether or not they should be authorized by the denomination, has a long history. The further development of multi-congregation situations and the overstretching of stipendiary clergy with sole charge make them almost essential. There may be a tension about shared oversight, as the church council and ministry team do not always consist of the same people.

Teaching, liturgical development, non-eucharistic services, Messy Church and other emerging forms are easier to introduce here. In a negative way, congregation members may perceive the team as a 'clique' or a closed group around the minister.

On the positive side, the strength of such situations comes with the acknowledgement that the full-time minister should not be expected to do everything. It develops the discussion about what a full-time minister is there for and the extent to which their ministry is priestly rather than administrative. It begins to allow for the possibility of the discernment of differing ministries and the need for appropriate training.

3 One priest with ordained assistants and other licensed ministers and several or many congregations

This presents one of the more complex situations and reflects piecemeal planning and pragmatic amalgamations. Clergy may have been appointed for any number of reasons and be at very different stages in their ministry. Specialist ministers and those in non-congregational settings may be engaged in pioneer ministries. The closeness of lay leaders to the principal minister may be – or feel – threatened.

The advantage of a greater staff to congregation ratio is that differences in liturgical traditions and innovation can be accommodated. The element of mission can be emphasized and a range of training opportunities and spirituality programmes can be offered. Within this level of staffing lies the capacity to engage with local community issues in a meaningful way with staff dividing up agreed areas of responsibility. The sense may be strong that this is a transitional arrangement which just happens to work; the appointment of a personality which does not fit would mean that the whole arrangement could be brought into jeopardy.

4 One priest with too many congregations to offer overall joint coverage, with areas subdivided

Midway between sole charge and a level of stipendiary staffing are situations where up to 20 congregations can find themselves with only one allocated stipendiary priest. It is not reasonable to expect all congregations to relate to one another, to travel far for worship or to join in one another's events. Sensible solutions are found locally. Congregations may well have been in local group-ings already, which are now amalgamated into a larger unit. There may be retired ministers in auxiliary roles and it is likely that shared worship with other denominations occurs on a fairly regular basis.

One stipendiary giving oversight to such a large area and group-ing can cause problems. Local and sub-group identities grow in importance. Coping strategies begin to emerge. Local pastoral care can be offered in a variety of authorized and informal ways and new systems are formed. Cooperation between churchwardens and the full-time minister will be paramount. Retired clergy, self-supporting ministers, readers and authorized lay workers constitute a significant local presence. Some form of coordination or whole group administration is essential.

5 One priest with overall local oversight, with ordained assistants with subdivisions for pastoral oversight

One creative opportunity presented by large groupings with enough staff is formal, internally agreed subdivision, which can provide manageability and reflect local identity. Local oversight by the senior stipendiary and oversight team become paramount. Stipendiary ministers, whether full or part time, devolve responsi-bility to other authorized ministers for a subdivision of the whole group. Trust of a different kind becomes evident. The full-time senior minister is present at agreed meetings and events and is the ultimate point of reference.

This type of subdivision means that local pastoral care can be provided, as can continuity for liturgical innovation and develop-ment. The exchange of experience is made possible through regular meetings of the wider clergy group and through their presence in overall leadership team or council meetings.

The role of the senior priest has to be worked at to prevent marginalization and the sense that an old 'parochial' system is being perpetuated, with those with devolved oversight taking full responsibility. The concept of local *episkope* or oversight can explain and support this role.

6 One united benefice or area containing former independent parishes in a new structure with perhaps a minister with overall local oversight, other clergy, readers, specialist staff, an executive administrator and other office staff

In this new situation the sense of local ownership can be difficult to achieve. Decisions can feel distant and remote from a particular local need. The subject of finance creates a sense of ownership within a congregation, and when the management of this is removed it is a great challenge to maintain necessarily high levels of local giving. Growth can feel threatened unless communication is extremely good, and those with administrative responsibilities need to retain their 'human' touch.

The weight of meetings and administration is lifted through this arrangement. One overall church council or church board has the responsibility for oversight of all congregations, for the management of finances and the care of buildings. The old local system of congregational responsibility for everything disappears, and the burden of multiplied administration and meetings for full-time stipendiary clergy is lifted. Time may be freed up for pastoral, evangelistic and social action outreach. Specialist care of buildings may be available, and perhaps expertise in fundraising and making applications for grant aid. If the new grouping reflects the character of a locality and has schools and other organizations in common, then a meaningful piece of work will have been done.

7 The deanery is the unit for local oversight configured in any number of ways

It was noted above that John Tiller predicted the deanery would become the ultimate unit for the local church. This oversight is located in an existing and recognized unit with established ways of relating to the diocese and the wider Church.

In a deanery grouping decisions can be made about the deployment of full-time stipendiary clergy. Hierarchy is avoided, since the role of dean can rotate around the clergy. Cooperation is of the essence. Parochial or congregational identity remains intact.

Control of finances and care for buildings remain with the congregation unless voluntarily ceded to a larger grouping. The responsibility for growth can be shared between congregation, groupings of congregations and the whole deanery.

Clergy and authorized clerical and lay ministers may have specialist responsibilities across a deanery. There may be a joint financing of specialist children's, family and other ministries. Pioneer ministries can receive adequate support through colleague-ship.

8 A 'minster' concept, where one large town-centre church is dominant, with strong musical and civic traditions, and a number of 'satellite', formerly independent, congregations

Some local situations require a specific solution or grouping. Where there is a large and perhaps dominant building with a distinctive set of ministries, colleagueship with smaller and more local congregations has the potential to be problematic.

Specialisms and local distinctiveness become important in such situations. Any sense of competitiveness or rivalry needs to be mitigated. One way to achieve this is for each local congregation to become a 'centre of excellence'. Minster situations are more likely to occur in market towns or larger urban areas where trad-itions of churchmanship or social service may be well established.

The oversight by the senior minister needs to avoid the impres-sion that they are primarily concerned with the larger building or congregation. Work within designated roles is essential. Clergy may have experience in a particular area, perhaps a preference for a small congregation, or, if they have choral or other musical skills, for the larger building and its activities.

Large buildings offer the opportunity to hold special events, and these are to be encouraged. For large buildings which do not have large congregations, the grouping of churches of one denom-ination in a town offers a wider range of voluntary support.

9 Congregations voluntarily joining in 'clusters', some of which will be geographical, others for specialist work and support

A great amount of innovation and creative endeavour is possible within this radical and non-geographical new network. Here congregations group or associate themselves with others according to interest or pastoral provision. Congregations wanting to develop youth work, for example, or confirmation preparation, or provide bereavement counselling, can combine according to commonly expressed need. One advantage of such 'non-geographical clustering' is that no one need feel pressurized into doing what a majority in a territorial grouping decide. Networks can flourish.There is likely to be a strong sense of directional leadership.

Organic growth can feel fulfilling but dispersed collegiality can reflect division. There is a danger that congregations of a like-minded persuasion – for example charismatic renewal, or with distinctive churchmanship – may band together. This may happen in congregations where the ministry of women is less welcome. These drawbacks are unlikely to prevent cooperation in most aspects of congregational development, however, and such an oversight solution may work and give community identity when other groupings appear inappropriate or impossible to achieve.

Reluctant change

Against these potentially confusing situations, two factors dominate. The first is how to sustain an effective local presence in each community. The second is how to encourage change given the recalcitrant nature of congregational life, as described by Maddy Thung in her European study (Thung, 1976). It is difficult to know which of these two factors should have priority – or if they are so interconnected that they provide an answer to this dilemma within themselves.

There is no doubt that local identity is strong in the analysis of how communities are built and sustained. Frequently the presence of a local church building and the contribution of its congregation are seen as important if not vital. The recalcitrant congregation is rightly defensive of its identity and wary of interference by outside bodies. The tensions within churches relating to a balance of power have already been described. In participative democracies there is now an inherited expectation that local opinion has a share in decision-making. Episcopally structured churches by their very nature and history have an inbuilt problem with this. The bishop and the accompanying hierarchy with synodical and legal structures have good reason to be there, but have to make essential adaptations which will enable local Christian communities to feel that they are members of a reciprocal partnership.

In this new situation of 'managing the present' in multi-congregation units, resentment about what was once local and familiar being taken away cannot be avoided. The fact that this means of coverage with locally based clergy did not produce effective missionary and community-building expertise is rarely acknowledged. Laypeople who support their local church have often yet to be persuaded of the benefits of larger groupings, or that they can find the provision of liturgical and sacramental ministries every Sunday many times over within their grouping. A colleague doing research in this situation reproduced the essence of an interview with one congregation member: 'Why should I travel 10 miles to join another small congregation also struggling to maintain hardly adequate worship when I can travel the same distance to a large church or even cathedral where something more substantial and nurturing can be found?'

Managing the present in these and other ways which are relevant to particular situations can seem daunting enough. Indeed, the multiplicity of local and small-scale tasks can create enormous busyness and lead to burnout and exhaustion. Clergy participating in leadership courses can fail to implement ideas or carry out good resolutions because they are immediately overcome by busyness when they return to their congregations. That is why the two sections which follow are essential if the new patterns of life in local congregations, grouped in new and challenging ways, are to be sustained.

Nurture identity

Team ministries frequently work to create a corporate identity. They give themselves a name, design a logo and create publications with a masthead in order to proclaim who they are. Group ministries operate in a similar way, often with more limited success at attempting to define a corporate identity. When much larger groupings are created, something more than window-dressing is required to establish a regional or larger sense of identity. Convenience has often dominated over a sense that an existing community identity has been recognized. Some congregations may feel that all they have in common is that they share one full-time minister. What else is it that they might expect from shared oversight?

The first response to this question has to be that these are the groupings, often among others, of a denomination of Christians in a locality. The primary element of identity for a multi-congregational grouping is its denominational ethos. Choices made have to be consistent with the national and international identity of the denomination. But denominations are also changing and adapting their identity, often driven by cultural and internal pressures. Within this, some policy changes – about the ministries of women, about baptism and admission to communion, about child protection and safeguarding, for example – will be made beyond the boundaries of the grouping but will affect all local congregations.

Arising from this are many local identity questions which need to be explored and may then lead to the formation of policy and the allocation of local resources. The first of these local decisions concerns the nature of collaboration expected between congregations. If the grouping is thought to have an air of permanence about it then a council or oversight committee should be formed to plan with the authorized ministers. Work to establish and resource a core of common identity needs to flow from this group.

If the desire to develop corporate oversight and a common identity is absent, fragmentation may occur, or the opportunity given not to be a congregation actively committed to the new situation. Representatives may come to meetings more to 'block' change than to facilitate it. Unhelpful or inappropriate behaviour may lead to a souring of the atmosphere and much energy may have to be spent in reconciliation and in attending to dysfunctional attitudes. Small and trusting steps need to be taken before the goodwill to bring in major changes can exist.

Identity is a deeply theological concept. It is about knowing who we are and who God is calling us to be or to become. It is a calling to every individual and to communities to move on from one form of life to another. The adaptation of identity for many denominations takes a step forward as women are appointed to leadership roles at local, regional or national level. The Revd Jane Day has written about how she experienced becoming a regional minister in the Baptist Church:

> One year into my Regional Minister role I began to wonder why I found leadership difficult, and observed that I exercised my leadership differently to my (mostly male) colleagues. I experienced a difference in the way I chaired meetings or the way I solicited information from others. I experienced frustration when I adopted a more collaborative and empowering style of leadership and my colleagues went ahead and made decisions without consultation. I also observed the use of exclusively male language despite me asking for an inclusive use of the Bible to be used at various events. These examples need further reflection as different styles may not always relate to gender, although my experience is that they probably do. (Day, 2013, p. 2)

In such situations it has to be possible to wait and watch and listen; the call from God to create new identities for the Church needs to be a shared experience. Shared identity both draws people and groups together and establishes an infectious sense of belonging which entices others to want to join them.

Create the future

It is the local church, in these new groupings of congregations, which is already creating future shapes of the Church. In time they may come to change the ethos and nature of our denominations. The task of the denomination remains significant: to give wider oversight, to relate to regional and national institutions, to provide resources for local development work and to work with other churches in international cooperation. It should aim to protect overburdened local ministers from hostile situations and dominant local personalities. It is the place where complaints can be balanced and appropriate procedures decided upon.

We do not know what the shape of a future local church will be, although we have some indication through the changes which have already taken place. One driver of change has been a decline in the number of stipendiary ministers; another has been the increasing cost of maintaining a national and a local church. Both factors, which relate to a change in pastoral provision and an increased sense of proprietorial ownership, were described earlier in my introductory picture of a church in the process of renewing itself. There is much farther to go.

What has to be avoided is short-termism, the idea that the present situation is temporary and that something of the 'old days' will return. That is now demonstrably not the case. Newness comes with the excitement of creating a future Church which will be more effective in its apostolic charge than churches of recent generations. Newness in church life comes slowly and after trial and error. The experiments with team and group ministries, with the learning which has emerged from them, perhaps, informs most current, often less formal developments. Changes in the understanding of priesthood and an increase in the expectation of 'shared' ministries form current drivers of change.

Much has been learned about the importance of continuity and succession in the consolidation of change. Most frustrating is the imposition of short-term strategies and the lack of local connectedness with mission initiatives devised at a distance by denominations. It has become evident that an emphasis on outreach to the unchurched or those on the fringes of the church has grown in local and national significance. This emphasis on 'mission' has led to a range of initiatives which deepen faith and welcome newcomers. These developments are creating identity and are giving a new sense of direction for local churches.

With this kind of change already taking place across groupings of congregations the question emerges about the kind of leadership which will be needed. What kind of training should be provided for ministers with these new responsibilities? Can and should the responsibilities once combined in one ministerial role now be divided? These changes may be a part of the future. The role and work of pastoring, of the priesthood and spiritual direction and of the missioner may well come to be seen as separate. Already the roles are becoming divided even if on occasion combined in one person. A diocese recently placed an advertisement describing the new full-time minister as 'Vicar and leader of the Mission Team'. Newness, born of necessity, may shake some foundations.

It is important to recognize that this is not a prediction of what a church might be like; it is a description of what the church in many places has already become. Every local congregational situation should be aware of the four messages contained in this chapter: the past with its stories has to be heard; the present has to be managed but with reflection and vision; the emerging identity of local Christian communities has to be established, and this across the new multi-congregational groupings which already exist; and a new future has to be created which has as its essence the principles of reciprocal oversight within caring local communities. The importance of emphasizing the nurturing of identity and creating the future is that this enables a revisiting of the core activities to put into perspective why we are so caught up in managing the present. We need to understand the distinction between what is 'core' and what is habitual or customary in our frenzied activity.

There is a pressing need to continue with an exploration of the theology of what it means to be part of a church which is undergoing continuing change. This has an immediate consequence for the nature of vocation – what God is calling us all to be – within these new communities and what kind of formation is to be developed which will call and nurture ministerial oversight in a future generation. A detailed exploration of why reciprocal oversight is such a fundamental concept rediscovers and polishes the lost jewel and determines the identity of a faith community.

3

Faith in Oversight

It is essential to explore how in the life and activities of grouped local congregations a much stronger sense of 'local ownership' can exist which can become a creative driving force for change. Distinctive styles of worship can flourish and the experiences of experiment exchanged. There may be an excitement in feeling invited to join or to become a 'learning community'. The local characteristics of a village, suburb or market town can rise to the surface. These have the overriding advantage of enabling local issues and interests to be reflected in prayerfulness, in worship, in the uses and development of the church building, and in community service. Two of my colleagues, Mark and Clare Sanders, reflect on the nature of local and multi-congregation ministries in *Growing Benefices ... and How to Survive Them*. They say, particularly about the rural church but equally for all, that we begin with three 'assets' or inheritances from the past: our parishes, our ministries and our buildings. Each in their own way can help us to fulfil our call to mission (Sanders and Sanders, 2013).

Many advantages can be discovered by being part of a multi-congregation grouping. This chapter falls into two parts and explores historical and theological perspectives. The first part examines the history of oversight in our churches, and the second presents an examination of the ways in which recent ecumenical agreements have added to our understandings of the exercise and potential of oversight. When combined these begin to give the framework of a theology which is necessary to enable congregations, their ministers and their denominations to move on from pragmatic restructuring towards a deeper understanding of what God is calling the Church to become for the future.

There are also disadvantages in multi-congregation situations, and these require a revision of inherited pastoral and vocational approaches to local ministry. The most serious for members of a congregation may be that the absence of a resident minister can produce 'drift' or a lack of overall direction. While the possibility is always present, there is a greater chance that dominant groups or personalities control local worship and activity, prevent new-comers from joining the inner decision-making groupings in a congregation and attempt to 'freeze' activity in a past view of what church life should be like. A sense of disconnectedness may be felt and even an impression that the minister favours one con-gregation over another. These inherent limitations to growth can be mitigated by structured and supported spiritual and inter-personal work with other local congregations.

A significant element in the dynamics of change, just as in single-minister congregations, concerns the uses and the balance of power. Tensions and sub-groups exist in every congregation. When change is proposed, or when security and continuity are threatened, these tensions come to the surface. They are evident in relationships with the wider Church. Proposals to create multi-congregation groupings or to increase the size of a grouping by merger or by adoption rarely come from a local initiative, but from restructuring proposals by a denomination. As outlined in Chapter 1, the financial pressures put on a congregation can increase a proprietorial attitude and lead to demands for a sig-nificant say in any proposed changes, as well as in the choice of minister and decisions about the 'work' or kind of ministry they will exercise. At this stage in an examination of a new situation, there is perhaps a greater reflective question than those about the balance of power between local, regional or national governance. It asks in which ways can the Christian gospel be developed for the future and lived within and by these newly reconfigured local communities. In attempting to answer this question it is import-ant to look at what kind of oversight and what kind of local ministries Christian communities need when they are brought into relationship with one another.

The significance of oversight

The New Testament and letters from the early successors of the apostles provide primary sources through which we can understand fundamental characteristics for effective Christian oversight within the first congregations. Deacons, presbyters and bishops are mentioned as local officials alongside prophets who had a more roving brief. In these first decades there is no precise evidence for how authorized ministries became regularized across the emerging churches.

In the Greek empire an *episkopos* was a state official appointed to 'see over' a city or region on behalf of others. In the Hebrew tradition the word describes a God who 'sees over' by visitation or the exercise of authority in a way which will cause change by bringing blessing or punishment. In the Bible judgement occurs in Jeremiah 6.15 and Isaiah 29.6, while blessing is given in Genesis 50.24–25 and Isaiah 23.16. A word like oversight can have less positive connotations: an oversight is something forgotten which should have been remembered and in Victorian England overseers were rather dictatorial middle-managers in industrial 'sweat shop' factories. There were also 'Overseers of the Poor', administering the Poor Law of England and the Workhouses which were the last resort of the poor, the orphaned and the destitute.

The term and office of *episkopos* does not arise in a direct and traceable way from the ministry of Jesus. The Dutch theologian Edward Schillebeeckx, in *Ministry: A Case for Change*, says, 'Apart from apostleship or "the apostolate", the Christian communities did not receive any kind of church order from the hands of Jesus when he still shared our earthly ministry' (1981, p. 5). Controversy continues over the variety of ways in which the early texts can be interpreted.

Setting out on what became a foundational exploration of the origins and nature of Christian ministry in his first substantial book, *The Gospel and the Catholic Church*, Michael Ramsey states:

Discussions of the primitive ministry have filled a large place in modern theological literature. The adherents of almost every post-reformation Church-system have sought to prove that their own form of ministry has the sanction of the New Testament, and the debates have often been tedious. Hence many welcomed with relief the conclusion reached by Dr Streeter in his book, *The Primitive Church* – that there was a great variety of forms of ministry in the Apostolic age, that there was no single type of Church order and that in the words of *Alice in Wonderland*, 'everybody has won and all shall have prizes'. (Ramsey, 1936, p. 68)

Since there remain possibilities for further interpretation of oversight in our own time, perhaps we can claim another prize! One gain in exploring what God might be asking in an exploration of this new situation of local oversight in multi-congregation ministries is to appreciate, maybe for the first time, the richness contained within the foundational concept of oversight in the earliest Christian communities.

As an accompaniment to practical experiment we need theological and organizational reflection on what is happening. History, practice and theology have to be brought together in new and dynamic ways. This can lead to a renewed or different interpretation of what the work of denominations and dioceses, of senior leaders and bishops might look like. Interpretations of types of church leadership, as with oversight, have changed along with developments in cultures and national means of governance. Churches have borrowed from and contributed to these developments.

The first phase of church order

For an understanding of how the local church became established in many parts of Northern Europe, and its purpose culturally determined, we need to look to the first Christian leaders and bishops. These were missioners continuing an apostolic commission. It was only later that they became consolidators and administrators and members of an elite ruling class. According to the Venerable Bede, the first chronicler and historian of the English Church, it was Pope Gregory I who sent Augustine (d. 604) as the first missionary bishop to England in 597. His mission was to convert the King (Ethelbert), who then allowed missionaries to preach in his kingdom of Kent. Augustine had a difficult time establishing his mission alongside the Christians who already existed across Britain: the 'Celtic' Church had local leaders who were descendants of the first Christians in the time of the Roman Empire.

Most important for the establishment of the local church was the work of the second bishop to be sent to Britain from Rome. Theodore of Tarsus (602–90) arrived in 669 to become Archbishop of Canterbury. It was Theodore who called the Council of Hertford in 672, and Bede states that Theodore was 'the first of the archbishops whom the whole English Church consented to obey'. He divided the existing dioceses, which corresponded to the English kingdoms. These boundaries are still recognizable today. In *Aspects of Anglican Identity*, Colin Podmore uses this historical occurrence to show that the dioceses were founded before the parishes and to this day determine the shape of the local church. He uses this argument from history to reinforce his view of a 'top-down' account of how ecclesiastical authority is established (Podmore, 2005).

As an administrator it was Theodore of Tarsus who first used the term 'parish' (Gk *paroikia*, from *para* = alongside, *oikos* = house) to mean the township where Christians resided and where a church had been built. In the earliest European settlements the Christianization of a community was related directly to the bishop and diocese. As Podmore suggests, it was the diocese which called the parishes into being and the bishop who appointed the clergy and administered discipline. It related the congregation to the community and the community to the wider Church. To the present day the tension between local parish and congregation and overseeing diocese with its bishop and staff continues. It is a relationship which is continually being renegotiated. This is another of those 'elephants' which is very real and which energizes much activity but is rarely spoken about. It is a part of the reconfiguring of the nature of national, especially episcopally ordered, churches. It reflects in a specific way fundamental questions which have to be brought out into the open. These concern local ownership and the location of a primary responsibility for ministry and mission. Consequent issues need to be re-examined about the kinds of regional and national oversight which are necessary and which serve as a continual reminder of membership of a national and international Church. The nature of the tradition represented by a denomination is also brought into question and where it is necessary to establish boundaries of faith and behaviour. One purpose of a regional and national presence is that it enables a denomination to maintain an informed and effective public face.

The purpose of ministry

The changes examined here, particularly in regard to multi-congregation ministries, are about the adaptation and development of church structures, and these have a long and distinctive history. It is not quite an 'adapt or die' situation but decline does bring its own warnings, particularly for those with wider responsibilities for oversight. They have to keep a strict distance from the exhaustion of 'managing the present' in order to oversee gradual but deliberate change. That churches in the historic denominations may not continue for ever was demonstrated by Ted Wickham in his research into church life in the industrial city of Sheffield:

> The weakness and collapse of the churches in the urbanized and industrialized areas of the country should be transparently clear to any who are not wilfully blind ... Yet many factors obscure the situation and so divert our serious attention from the problem. There is our acquiescent assumption of the English Church as an age-old and venerable institution, perdurable as the English weather, which will go down with the ages to the end of history ... which can veil the inertia of ancient institutions, and the fact

that 'churches' as distinct from the Church of Jesus Christ, can have historical beginnings and endings. (Wickham, 1957, p. 11)

While using informed and intuitive oversight in his analysis of a missionary situation Wickham was critical of existing Church structures. Despite his strong and individualistic stance he did not go on to explore how the causes of decline could be addressed through local reinterpretation or adaptation. Similar conclusions were reached in the Church of England report, *Faith in the Countryside* (1990). This report examined the complexities of multi-congregation ministries and used examples of good practice to point ways forward. These specific industrial and rural situations each have their own significance; alongside them are general features about the character of local church life which, in perverse ways, seem to transcend local setting and culture. John Drane, academic and radical critic of the experience of life in local congregations, maintains that the reasons for significant numbers leaving the Church do not relate to music, sermons or liturgy but to the poor level of relationships between members of congregations (Drane, 2008, p. 99).

Local ownership of ministry and mission

A modern-day prophet who addressed the question of how growth in local congregations could be owned was Roland Allen (1868–1947), although he went unheeded and unrecognized in his own time. From his experience in the mission field he argued that Christianity will never be owned by a people unless their leaders are indigenous and internally appointed, even if still overseen in some way by their wider Church. His principal argument was about leadership of local congregations, but it has equal application to regional, national and international churches. He returns our argument to the life of the early Church and the centrality of local appointments and the ways in which oversight is exercised. Initially his books were dismissed as the works of an eccentric, as if he was trying to diminish the work of mission agencies.

With the advent of more and more local ministry schemes and with the disenchantment concerning leadership appointed externally to a parish or diocese, his arguments are gaining increasing validity and force. In the introduction to the 1927 edition of *The Spontaneous Expansion of the Church*, Allen wrote:

> Many years ago my experience in China taught me that if our object was to establish in that country a church which might spread over the six provinces which then formed the Diocese of North China, that object could only be attained if the first Christians who were converted by our labours understood clearly that they could by themselves, without any further assistance from us, not only convert their neighbours, but establish churches. (Allen, 1962)

Without this rediscovery, the essential local ownership of a church by its priests and laypeople will be absent. In the following sections the reasons for this 'lack of ownership' by the people but not by their rulers will become clear.

Prophets such as Roland Allen frequently discern the signs of the times but also live ahead of a time when their warnings will be heard. What Allen wrote in the first two decades of the twentieth century is only now being taken seriously (and not everywhere) by those who want to see a very different balance of power and leadership in the Church:

> The Church cannot grow because we insist on a full-time professionally trained ministry as the essential leadership of the Church and the only means of the administration of the sacraments. Because such a ministry cannot be provided in sufficient quantity, the Church cannot expand ... Moreover, such a ministry, even where available, is not acceptable, for the Church feels that it has been imposed upon it and therefore does not belong to it. (Allen, 1962)

The important vocational question for this exploration of local ministry in multi-congregational settings is precisely the point made by Allen. How can the Church continue to expand when the traditional pattern of the full-time stipendiary is no longer available? How can local people, taking initiatives themselves, gain the confidence to spearhead the growth of their Christian community without the day-to-day support of a full-time minister?

Before moving into an examination of the practicalities of new ministries, it is necessary to describe two significant parts of an understanding of the nature of Christian ministries. The first concerns what can be rediscovered from the essential elements which emerge from our biblical and ecclesiastical traditions. These can then be developed with theological understandings to inform a whole range of oversight ministries. The second concerns the international ecumenical agreements of recent decades concerning the nature of the Church and the functions of its ministries. Without the following sections my exploration would run the risk of being another 'how to' book. We need to have a theological and an ecclesiological underpinning which will inform and strengthen our activities. All the historic denominations are undergoing a process of gradual and incremental change. What is changing also is the nature and content of the work of ministry and of the Church's ministers. Once this discussion is complete we will have the foundations for an understanding of the kind of vocation to ministry needed for a quite different kind of Church.

Oversight as relationship

We need to address the perpetual, but particularly modern, question of relationships in hierarchical organizations. This can be done in a new way through a rediscovery of one particular activity which has been both underused and misused through the centuries: the ancient rite of visitation. In many denominations the visitation of parishes is still an obligation – for diocesan staff, the chairs of Methodist Districts, Baptist regional officers, archdeacons, vicars general; it is an opportunity which bishops can take at any time. It can now become part of the role and responsibility of the minister with local oversight in a multi-congregation situation. If it is seen not as an 'inspection' but as a means of gaining information and to re-establish a sense of overall direction it is a privileged opportunity.

The activity of visitation can re-establish relationships between those with wider oversight and priest and congregation, and has significant theological underpinning with origins which reflect the very nature of God. The Greek version of the Old Testament, the Septuagint, calls God *episkopos* once, in Job 20.29, where the reference is to a judicial function. It is used in Judges 9.28 for officers, in 2 Chronicles 34.12 for supervisors of funds, and for overseers of priests and Levites in Nehemiah 11.9. All contact with God is understood as in some sense relational and expresses feelings that people are cared for, protected, led and disciplined. That visitation is understood as a two-way relationship, described as 'seeing over', is developed in the Hebrew phrase *Kol Yisrael arevim zeh la-zeh*, which means 'all Jews (or all the people of Israel) are responsible for one another'. Former Chief Rabbi Jonathan Sacks says that without a principle of collective responsibility – which means for leaders 'seeking the good of those you serve' – authority roles can become detached and misunderstood, creating separated groups of 'leaders' and 'followers'.

God was first experienced as a relational being who created humans to be 'a little lower than the angels' (Ps. 8.4). The creation stories and the giving of the Ten Commandments illustrate this (Gen. 1–3; Exod. 20). The experience of divine intervention can be described as a blessing or a curse or condemnation. When Joseph was about to die in exile with his people in Egypt he was confident that God would 'visit' the people in his charge and enable them to return to their homeland (Gen. 50.22–26).

The experience of the people in exile in Babylon in the time of Isaiah brought a similar response. There was a strong sense that their God still 'watched over' them, and even though they had strayed like 'a harlot' they would be protected and eventually return to their homeland (Isa. 23.16). There was also a sense that God's oversight brought judgement. Jeremiah prophesied that there would be a scattering of the people as a result of God's displeasure (Jer. 6.15). Isaiah's great vision of the potter and the clay concludes that it is within the power of the potter to destroy if there is dissatisfaction with what has been created (Isa. 29.16).

A development of this work of visitation has implications for the minister with overall responsibility for a large number of congregations. Supremely this is demonstrated in the 'little' visitation to Mary and the greater visitation in the intervention in history of the life, death and resurrection of Jesus. This visitation is described in particular as the opening of access to God for the 'gentile' peoples. The speech of James makes this clear (Acts 15.14). The establishment of a two-way relational basis for oversight as visitation, firmly established in the Old Testament and begun in a new way in the New Testament, goes some way to explain the heated controversies about the nature of acceptable authority. When the balance is tipped too much towards either hierarchical authority or local independence then a serious fault-line is revealed. Visitation can be the bridge between the local and the regional and national. It re-establishes the essential shepherd-like practice where leaders must know and be known by their people.

Oversight and the ability to manage boundaries

Another theological opportunity contained within the practice of oversight – an essential one in multi-congregation situations – concerns the ways in which oversight can enable communities to move forward. Liminality is a rather refined and technical term which has to fight for inclusion in an understanding of the work of oversight, particularly regarding the role of the bishop as a significant figure in the life of a community, region or nation. Liminality, in terms of social structure and time, is the state of being 'in between': individuals move from their known identity to another, formally recognized one with all the attendant personal and social transformation. It was developed as a modern concept by Victor Turner, who saw that groups, and whole communities, experience a 'time of uncertainty' as they move from one understanding of themselves to another (Turner, 1967).

For the leader with oversight responsibility, this sense of the need for someone to act as a legitimating agent in the facilitation of change can become pivotal. By their presence, or through public speech articulating what many think but dare not say, the authentication of change can be enabled. This aspect of the religious leader role was articulated well by Bruce Reed, founder of the Grubb Institute. In an essay on the development of understanding of the role of religious leaders for the organization MODEM he described the religious leader as a 'manager of boundaries' (Nelson, 1999, pp. 243–62).

There is strong biblical precedent for this concept. References to change through a liminal experience serve to give the oversight role theological authenticity. In his dream, Jacob found himself caught up between heaven and earth in a state of temporary suspension (Gen. 28.12–19). Isaiah at the time of his call, 'In the year that King Uzziah died ...', was transported in a temporary way by a heavenly experience before he was 'sent' to speak on the Lord's behalf (Isa. 6.1–16). In perhaps a more familiar way Simon was renamed Peter, 'the rock', at the beginning of his ministry as a disciple (Matt. 16.18).

From these two pieces of theological unfolding of the particular roles and opportunities within *episkope* and the biblical quarrying which has gone before it the time has now come to examine precisely how ministries of oversight are or can be exercised in multi-congregation situations. Much of this can be achieved by utilizing a route provided by the work and achievements of the ecumenical movement.

Oversight in ecumenical agreements

The next stage in an examination of the concept of oversight is to look at what denominations and congregations have received from ecumenical theology. This will help to give a shape to what is being put into effect locally in ministries of oversight. Initially, many people thought that these discussions between denominations were about mergers, and if they failed there was some disappointment with underlying divisions being brought to the surface. We are now in a position to see that the enduring legacy of these conversations and agreements is about new understandings of faith, ministerial practice and church. We can begin to harvest some of the fruits, and nurture the green shoots which are now growing from seed sown. The lasting theological and ministerial contribution from these discussions between denominations is the extent to which agreement about the nature of ministries, not least those of oversight, has been reached.

Across the denominations, all churches, however egalitarian, have some kind of authority and leadership structure. Much common ground in the understanding of ministries of oversight can be seen in the agreements which arise from ecumenical discussions over the past 50 years. They offer both theological and practical underpinning for ways in which denominations with their local congregations might establish more comprehensive understandings of oversight.

The foundation document for contemporary understandings of oversight is the result of an agreement made at Lima in Peru in 1982: *Baptism, Eucharist and Ministry (BEM)*, also known as the Lima Document. *BEM* has in its 'Ministry' section a major exploration of *episkope* (WCC, 1982), describing the origin of the term as oversight in the appointment of leaders in the first decades of the Church. Discussing contemporary interpretations of ministerial relationships in episcopally structured churches, it comments: 'the degree of the presbyter's participation in the episcopal ministry is still an unresolved question of far-reaching ecumenical importance' (*BEM*, p. 25). It is this uncertainty which allows the space I am attempting to fill to be occupied by the inclusion of local oversight in multi-congregation situations. The volumes edited by Max Thurian which chart the worldwide 'cultural', theological and ecclesiological responses to the Lima Document provide studies which analyse European churches as organizations in an essential international context (Thurian, 1987).

Understandings of oversight have been of increasing significance in the 60 years of conversations between the Anglican and

Methodist Churches. The nature of episcopal, apostolic govern-ance is also the principal concern of Nordic churches in their conversations with the Church of England; the *Porvoo Common Statement* of 1993 explores the need for new dialogue about *episkope* in some detail. The history of developing relationships between the Scandinavian and Baltic Lutheran churches and Anglicanism is charted by Lars Österlin. His foundational work describes generations of European contact and has been followed by a series of publications as the dialogue with other episcopal churches has developed (Österlin, 1995). Grace Davie has written a seminal text on the relationship of the European churches to the culture in which they are set (Davie, 2000). Conversations between the Church of England and the Roman Catholic Church focus in part on differences of interpretation about the apostolic nature of bishops' ministry and the transmission of authority within *episkope* (ARCIC, 1988).

The process of bringing these agreements into the life of the local church is called 'reception'. Those involved in the construc-tion of these agreements argue that this reception has been slow to happen (Avis, 2010). My view is that the absence of this internal-izing of the theological understandings of oversight has prevented much creative thinking about multi-congregation ministries. There was for many years an assumption that the principal purpose of ecumenical conversations was to achieve structural unity, and this clouded any broader conceptual understanding of oversight. Had the theological richness of the content of agreements been under-stood and acted on then a different kind of learning about shared oversight would have taken place. Interestingly, one strident commentator of this process, Monica Furlong, says in *The C of E: The State It's In*, 'The Church of England finds it easier and more rewarding to be ecumenical with Roman Catholics, Ortho-dox Christians and Methodists than to build bridges, however tenuous, within the different branches of its own family' (2000, p. 341). In multi-congregation ministries we find challenges both for congregations of the same denomination to build bridges of understanding with one another and also for congregations from differing traditions to grow in mutual understanding. In my definition, 'watching over one another in community' for the deepening of an understanding of a denomination's 'culture' and how it can renew its understanding of itself, oversight comes into its own.

The personal practice of oversight

The task now is to take the theological background, which suggests that the practice of oversight is essential in the work of any leader since it reflects the nature of God, and to translate what the work looks like into a structure providing formation and support. We can base this starting point not on opinion or emerging local experience but in the international context of understandings of ministry within churches. The source documents of ecumenical agreements made in the past 50 years command international respect, and those relating to the practice of ministry stem from the agreements described above: the Lima Document (*Baptism, Eucharist and Ministry*), *The Porvoo Common Statement*, the Anglican–Methodist Unity Commission and in the Anglican and the Lutheran Conversations with the Roman Catholic Church.

The essence of these agreements in regard to ministries in the Church need to be set out in detail as they present the basis of practical work and analysis which informs later chapters. First, before any denominational difference is acknowledged, there is an overriding understanding that the whole people of God sharing the Christian faith have a 'common life' together. This is exemplified in the word *koinonia*, and developed in the *Porvoo Common Statement* in the exploration of 'God's Kingdom and the Mystery and Purpose of the Church' (Section 5, p. 7). It locates its basis in 1 John 3, where Christians are called to share in a common life, *koinonia*.

The common thread running through all Christian ministries is that the leadership of present-day churches stems in a direct way from the work and ministry of the first apostles. Those who are called to ministry share a common calling to proclaim the message of Christianity and to guard its tradition. The concept used to describe this common calling is **apostolicity** and has been central in the content of Anglican–Methodist Conversations, the Porvoo Common Statement and in Anglican–Roman Catholic Dialogue.

Amid differences of interpretation of the nature of apostolic leadership and the consequences of historical division within the churches there remains one biblical and ecclesiological foundation. It is that of **unity**, represented in different ways within the one Body of Christ through the mutual recognition and acceptance of Trinitarian baptism. *BEM* states this common understanding which is the foundation of all further dialogue:

> Baptism is a sign and seal of our common discipleship. Christians are brought into union with Christ, with each other and with the Church of every time and place. Our common baptism, which unites us to Christ in faith, is thus a basic bond of unity. (*BEM*, p. 3)

The platform on which *BEM* and the ecumenical documents and agreements which precede and follow it can be said to stand is the ecclesiological and theological concepts held in common of *koinonia*, **apostolicity** and **unity**.

We also see in *BEM* the first and, for the practitioners of local oversight, key descriptions of the way in which this ministry is practised. Formative statements in *BEM* propose that the ministries of oversight are exercised in complementary ways, described as **personally, collegially** and **communally** (pp. 25–6). A ministry of oversight is **personal** because the presence of Christ among his people can most effectively be pointed to by the person ordained to proclaim the gospel and call the community to serve God in unity of life and witness (p. 26). Oversight is **collegial**, first because the bishop gathers together those who are ordained to share in the tasks of ministry and represent the concerns of the community, and second because through the collegiality of bishops the Christian community in local areas is related to the wider Church, and the universal Church to that community (p. 26). A ministry of oversight is **communal**, because the exercise of ordained ministry is rooted in the life of the community and requires the community's effective participation in the discovery of God's will and the guidance of the Spirit (p. 26).

These fundamental theological and ministerial statements can be put in diagrammatic form to produce a 'template' for an integrated understanding of oversight (see Figure 2). The descriptions so far are summarized, demonstrating the relationship and interdependence between each for a new understanding of oversight.

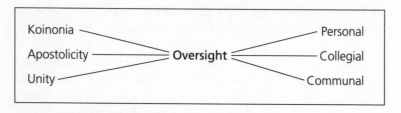

Figure 2 An integrated understanding of oversight

International responses

All European ecumenical debate about the theology of ministry is set in a world context. The *BEM* document was discussed by an astonishingly wide number of denominations from around the world. Their responses form a five-volume series published by the Faith and Order Commission of the World Council of Churches (Thurian, 1986). Some of these conclusions and responses are relevant to understanding history and culture as local ministry across a wide area is carried out.

In the Church of South India unique agreements were made in 1947 under which churches with differing understandings of *episkope* gave their consent to a unity scheme which was thought to be a possible model for other areas of former missionary endeavour. The four uniting churches – Anglican, Congregational, Presbyterian and Methodist – were able to accept the Lambeth Quadrilateral, including its fourth tenet which describes 'the historic episcopate locally adapted'. The Lambeth Quadrilateral was first agreed by bishops in the USA meeting in Chicago in

1886, and subsequently by the Lambeth Conference of Anglican bishops in 1888. The four points are: the Holy Scriptures contain all things necessary for salvation; acceptance of the Creeds, especially the Apostles and the Nicene; acceptance of the sacraments of baptism and Holy Communion; the historic episcopate locally adapted. I propose further 'local adaptations' of oversight which need to be understood as local cultural situations differ.

The Church of South India's response to *BEM* is significant as it raised questions about the 'cultural' link between the orders of deacon, priest and bishop and the element of hierarchy assumed between them. It echoes Roland Allen's comments about missionary work in China and the need for local ownership of mission and congregation building. Ministries of oversight can be perceived and acted on in different ways in various cultural settings, as Keith Elford has pointed out in his work on mergers and amalgamations. The response of the Church of South India saw in the call to ministry of all the baptized an equality which needed to be re-emphasized. It also asked important emerging questions for Christians in the West about how to live in obedience to Christ's call in a multi-religious and a multi-cultural situation.

Lutheran churches around the world also responded to *BEM*, and in the debate and analysis of the relationship of hierarchy to orders and *episkope* the Church of Sweden's response is representative. It reminded those committed to ecumenical debate that the tasks of the Church were not primarily about ministry but about word and sacrament. The Augsburg Confession was used as a doctrinal basis (Articles V, XIV and XXVVII), which maintains that the foundations of the Church are the proclamation of the gospel in word and sacrament. Their response was that God instituted ministry in order that the proclamation of the gospel may be enabled to function. Ultimately for them the tradition of continuity of apostolic teaching was more important than apostolic succession. These two responses to *BEM* offer an initial critique and an enriching reflection on the way in which a generally accepted report has to be received and nuanced by churches in various parts of the world, set in differing cultures each with a significant and distinctive ecclesial history. They ask culturally related questions about the significance of *episkope* without in any way diminishing its importance.

Ecumenical oversight and the local church

We can see that *koinonia*, **apostolicity** and **unity** are identified alongside what will become key components for the practice of oversight as **personal, collegial** and **communal**. It is now necessary to expand these understandings of key pieces of ecumenical theology in ways which relate all ministries to one another, giving an overall justification for the establishment of a way forward in order for all our churches to have a greater understanding of what it means to 'watch over one another in community'.

➢ **Koinonia.** Every characteristic of oversight must arise from the community within which it is expressed, and as a function from the calling of the 'whole people of God' (*BEM*, p. 20). Christianity, while being a faith which upholds and inspires the individual, has the basic tenet that faith only grows and is informed by membership of a wider group, which itself is part of an even wider community. The basis of this is the sacrament of baptism through which all Christians recognize one another as members of a common community of faith (*BEM*, pp. 2–3).

➢ **Apostolicity.** The ways in which a community of churches expresses its unity is that it adheres to internationally agreed characteristics and methods of ministry. These are based on understandings about the continuity of a commission begun and legitimized by the first apostles. Most significant for many denominations is that the structure of ordination and consecration of ministers can be traced back to the work of the apostles, themselves commissioned by Jesus during the time of his earthly ministry.

➢ **Unity.** Recent decades have been characterized by a search for structural unity between denominations. Ecumenical theologians see this search to be drawing to a close, and view it as a time when energy may have been misspent (Kasper, 2009;

Avis, 2010). However, the theological agreement achieved remains as an enduring legacy.

Personal and community roles within oversight

Wide-ranging theological issues which encapsulate international agreements need to be brought down to earth. The local minister, ministry team and congregations will ask important questions about their own roles and expectations. In the *BEM* and *Porvoo* agreements, and the Anglican–Methodist conversations, some key and unifying concepts emerge, giving answers to questions about the ways in which ministers understand their new vocational role and how congregations and local communities can share in the exercise of oversight. These descriptions expand how we as members of Christian congregations can 'watch over one another in community'.

Personal oversight

The very fact that *episkope* is expressed in the appointment of a person means that oversight will always be about people in relationship. This is the essence of my reassessment of the concept of visitation. *BEM* says: 'It is personal because the presence of Christ among his people can most effectively be pointed to by a person' (p. 25). Leadership is personal, but is always in relationship with other people and conducted in ways which reflect the needs and acceptable practices of the age.

The style of oversight has changed or is undergoing change in most parts of the world. The 'monarchical' style of episcopal leadership is no longer acceptable. Personal episcopal leadership and oversight requires the consent of the people who make up the Church. The second report of the Anglican–Methodist conversations (2001) reminds us that the personal office of oversight is not carried out in a completely individual way: 'The personal dimension presupposes the collegial and the communal, complementing them and upholding them' (p. 25). Three significant working understandings emerge for all those engaged in local ministries but especially in large groupings of congregations: that oversight is exercised personally, collegially and communally (see Figure 3).

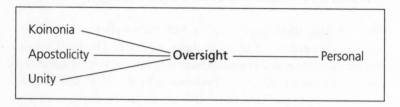

Figure 3 Personal oversight

Collegial oversight

In almost all churches, and certainly those within the historic denominations, leaders at various levels operate as a group in relation to one another. This needs to be done in the essential relationship church leaders have with their clergy and laypeople as they meet together in synods. Those with multi-congregation responsibilities may well need to learn to relate to their bishop, archdeacon or district chair in more personal ways. The purpose of meeting together in this reconfigured way will be to try to achieve a new kind of reciprocal relationship.

Is it possible to define what collegiality actually means? We are fortunate that Mary McAleese, Emeritus Professor of Law and former President of the Irish Republic, has made a study of the uses of the word. With a lawyer's precision she concludes with a summary definition:

At its simplest, the idea of collegiality is rooted, however vaguely, in the notion of a college. It suggests a gathering of individuals into a common association or grouping ring-fenced in some identifiable way. (McAleese, 2012, p. 25)

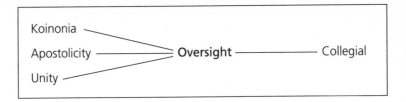

Figure 4 Collegial oversight

Communal oversight

Trust cannot be achieved unless those expressing and exercising leadership represent the changing expectations in the communities where they exercise their jurisdiction. All ministers represent tradition, and one characteristic by which they act with integrity is that they are aware of and are formed by their own tradition. Their ministry arises from the faith and traditions of the communities which have shaped and chosen them. But communal means much more than that today. *BEM* says, 'It is communal, because the exercise of ordained ministry is rooted in the life of the community and requires the community's effective participation in the discovery of God's will and the guidance of the Spirit' (p. 25).

A basis in the combination of tradition, theology and ministerial practice for the practice of oversight has now been established. It has been expanded, explained and dwelt on at some length in order to emphasize the contribution of ecumenical discussions which would otherwise run the risk of being shelved and forgotten. These agreements about the nature of ministries of oversight are a treasure to be savoured, equally for the local church and multi-congregation ministries as for senior appointments. They need now to be related to what the actual work of ministry and oversight looks like when applied to the leadership of teams and groups. The next stage in my exploration and reconstruction of *episkope* as oversight has now to be related to the ways in which oversight is described in organizational thinking.

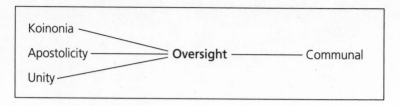

Figure 5 Communal oversight

Oversight in multi-congregation ministries

The conclusion of this chapter brings me to a point where I am able to say that my choice of the exploration of the essence of the Church and how understandings can be expanded strengthens the basic need that we have to learn again how to 'watch over one another in community'. We are at a place where something new and exciting can emerge, and in that case there has to be theological, ecumenical and practical coherence, grounded in an integrity which will stand up to criticism and reflect immediate need.

A further exploration follows to see whether it is possible to establish theological and ecclesiological descriptions of what can fill a liminal 'space in between' for a new understanding of *episkope*. This should be faithful to an original charism, reflect a continuing apostolic commission and meet an immediate pastoral and vocational need. It will be possible to achieve this aim, not in a comprehensive way, but by using 'building blocks' which can be put in place to form the structure for a significant development in the justification and use of *episkope* as oversight.

A human and a divine institution

Oversight has as its justification the responsibility to guide and lead in community. This relationship to the Creator God, who called faith into being and believers into the community of the Church, which is the Body of Christ, means that the responsibility of the overseer to be the 'good shepherd' includes a commitment to accompany others across real boundaries. The emergence of the concept of mission has been noted in ordinals and in descriptions of the work of ministries of oversight. The changing nature of how mission is understood has been observed. Is the aim of mission primarily to establish and renew the place and influence of Christianity in the transformation of societies, or is it to win adherents and enrol them as members in a more discernible community from which they will be equipped for service in the world? This joining together of theological and practical ideas attempts through experience and reflection to enable the depth and richness contained within the concept of oversight to be embraced in new and affirming ways.

The broader, unifying concept of oversight proposed here has the potential to give a renewed sense of community and identity to churches in great danger of further fragmentation and division. It forms the theological basis for ministries of oversight in multi-congregation situations.

Although historic agreements between and within denominations have provided major understandings of the nature of the Church's ministry, none have been integrated and absorbed into the life of national and local churches. This chapter has offered a link which is both theoretical, based on theological understandings of the nature of oversight, and practical, providing ecclesiological and vocational motivation for the practice of ministry. Such an integrating theology is essential to inform and support those already called to positions of responsibility and authority. It can be applied to the discernment of vocation and the subsequent identification of those yet to be appointed, and perhaps be used as a means of establishing criteria for those who encourage or discern vocation to these ministries. It is essential in the consolidation of new patterns of ministry that those involved are able to learn in new ways what it means to be able to 'watch over one another in community'.

4

Multi-Congregation Leadership

In multi-congregation ministries the needs and gifts of ministry exercised by differing individuals come into their own. Delegation within trusting relationships is essential and is often the result of hard work. It involves the establishment of roles and the maintenance of clear and agreed boundaries of responsibility. Just as there is not one ideal structure for congregations grouped together, so there is no one ideal type of leader. We have observed that understood difference becomes of the very greatest significance when the needs, histories, church cultures and social structures of congregations are taken into account. A theological underpinning of the work of ministry has been provided in the discussion of recent ecumenical agreements which define oversight roles both locally and internationally.

Throughout this chapter there is the opportunity to work in a creative way with the words and images used for leaders and leadership. Further personal resources can be revealed in order to manage the present while nurturing identity and creating and shaping the future. To begin with, the ways in which personality affects leadership and enables it to take different forms are set out. It may well be that a particular kind of leadership is needed at the stage of development a congregational grouping feels it has reached. It is important to look at what writers on church life and ministry say about leadership within oversight in order to determine the emerging understandings about the nature of ministry. It will then be possible to put together views about the needs within congregations and to propose some generic oversight 'models' or concepts.

The difficult question of ambition needs to be addressed in this chapter about leadership. Christians should be uneasy about the kind of ambition which strives more than anything else to get a person 'to the top', yet our very nature contains an element of the Creator God and this should be recognized. It means that we want a sense of fulfilment in all that we do. There is a vocational element also. Few people put themselves forward for ministry because they think they might be good at running a large organization. This in itself presents a problem, since in the selection process the reasons given to support a vocation and the criteria used by vocations advisers and those who select potential clergy may well not match the tasks and roles candidates would be asked to perform after ordination or being licensed to authorized lay ministry. It is therefore more appropriate for Christians to embrace achievement rather than ambition in any walk of life. It is also important that this achievement is not gained at the expense of others or at an enormous cost to family or to personal integrity.

Multi-congregation stipendiary ministries of oversight are *not* about creating 'super czars' who will oversee large groupings of congregations, nor are they about sharing out the work done by fewer ministers. Rather they are about those in local congregations developing an agreed way of working within given roles, building new visions together and, supremely, developing the kind of trust which will allow a new kind of local Christian presence to emerge and be sustained in local communities. In addition, new and quite different collegial relationships can be forged with those who oversee denominations at regional or national levels. With their significant if largely unrecognized expertise in this area, churches are developing experience to share with others as well as learning from it themselves.

Leadership within oversight

Leadership as an activity within oversight needs to be defined and explained. The word 'leader' comes from the Old English *lædan*, which has meanings suggesting travelling together, guiding and making pathways through to a new place. These are ideas and concepts of people using their inner resources, joint efforts and collective wisdom to develop their life as a community. Throughout history leadership has been concerned with ways of giving an individual or a group responsibility for creating and achieving a desired future. Team leadership joins ancient and new definitions together because it talks about a people making a journey together.

In Africa, interpretations of leadership illustrate richness and the possibility of difference in application from a common root. John Sentamu, Archbishop of York, has said that in his original language of Luganda leadership has a number of connected meanings:

> The word *omukulembeze* can mean the one who goes before; a pioneer; the one who clears the forest; the one who clears a path or who builds a bridge for others to cross the river.

Using another African example, Peter Price, a former Bishop of Bath and Wells, illustrates the need for strategic leadership and the difference between types of leader and the gifts and expectations they bring to their work:

> An African proverb observes that, 'The one who builds the path cannot make it straight'. Sometimes leadership is misunderstood as path-building, and many church leaders lose their way because, instead of mapping out where the path should lead, they spend too much time trying to build it. (Price, in Nelson, 2004, p. 163)

Working together in ministry

The personality, leadership style and effectiveness of any individual or group will depend ultimately on the stage of development or decline of the organization, whether company, charity or church, to which they belong. This 'situation' is often described by the concept of a life cycle. Charles Handy uses it in his development of the rather technically termed 'sigmoid curve' (Handy, 1995, pp. 49f.). It charts what is sensed by intuitive leaders or reformers, which drives them to initiate change (see Figure 6).

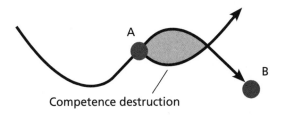

Competence destruction

Figure 6 The sigmoid curve

His key idea is that leaders need to capture a new and energizing concept while the 'success' curve is still in its ascendance, at point A. When leaders attempt to renew in the 'decline' arc of the curve (B), this will be associated with the experienced aspects of failure. Elements of death and resurrection can be seen here; the divine acts of intervention in the renewal events take their origin from the life, death and resurrection of Jesus Christ. Timely intervention, informed by intuition and experience, is of the essence in the theology of renewal and the necessary encouragements and restraints which characterized the life of the Christian Church in its first decades. The appropriateness of intervention leading to renewal has been one aspect of the challenging leadership role which accompanies the life and writings of reformers.

In any organization every group and individual member is at a different stage in the 'life cycle'. This is particularly true of the congregations within any kind of grouping, and it is essential to have some knowledge of where each is in its 'life cycle'. The Alban Institute has pioneered research into how congregations work and interact with their ministers so that illusions generated by over-optimistic leaders can be punctured. Working within the Alban, Martin Saarinen has taken the sigmoid curve concept and applied it to the life cycle of a congregation. His categories are: birth, infancy, adolescence, prime, aristocracy, bureaucracy and death. At various points in the growth–decline continuum within congregations, dioceses and denominations there are places where 'green shoots' of growth are emerging, thus linking the sigmoid and life-cycle concepts (Saarinen, 1986, 1996). Even within one congregation different groups will be at their own stage in this life cycle. Teamwork and constant reference to the oversight of the team leader can help to identify these. Groups whose existence cannot and should not continue need the authoritative advice and support of the minister with oversight of local leaders in order to make difficult decisions about how the work and life of an ailing group should be ended. In multi-congregation situations managing or overseeing development applicable to the stage in the life cycle of a congregation is a most sensitive matter. When misjudged it can add to the resentments described earlier in the 'memory' of a congregation, and to ammunition for those already disposed to oppose such a grouping of congregations.

If a situation is judged correctly then energy can be released and a great sense of well-being engendered. The language of balance and strategy in team oversight has been developed by John Adair and used to support and encourage church leaders in their attempts at an understanding of comprehensive oversight. His Venn diagram showing the interaction between team, task and individual needs (Adair, 2002, p. 76) has become a template for oversight (see Figure 7).

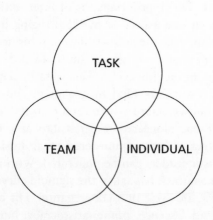

Figure 7 Task, team and individual leadership

Adair's work on group leadership has become foundational for those who offer consultancy to church groups and their leaders. In this threefold attempt at a balance in collaborative and team leadership, some see a parallel with the Trinitarian nature of God, although there is a danger in seeing in any threefold construction something of the nature of God. What can be established and developed is the fundamental concept of the need to balance both complementary and competing demands in the exercise of oversight to produce something which is greater and more effective than the sum of its parts.

Meredith Belbin's description of team and group roles with their constituent components each offering a particular contribution is significant here. The great advantage of his work is that it keeps the focus on task while identifying relevant team roles. In the late 1960s Belbin and his team of researchers based at the Henley Management College studied the behaviour of managers from all over the world over a number of years (www.belbin.com). Clusters of behaviour were identified as underlying successful work in teams, and these effective traits were given names. First eight and then nine individual characteristics were identified, and from these emerged team roles within shared oversight.

John Adair uses task, team and individual to illustrate that all need to be accompanied into further growth, that they need to share in giving an organization a sense of direction and that authoritative oversight is needed to recall them to the overall task. Gillian Stamp presents similar concepts when she refers to team leadership and oversight as requiring the activities of 'tasking, tending and trusting'. Again, tending enables team members to grow, tasking gives the sense of direction, and trusting expresses the need for authoritative oversight (www.gillianstamp.com). Each activity is not always equally necessary, and experience suggests that they need to be balanced according to circumstances and the strengths and weaknesses of the particular group or individual (see Figure 8).

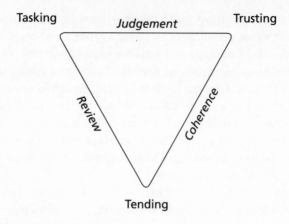

Figure 8 The tripod of work

The idea that some universal or generic categories are emerging is reinforced by Thomas Downs. In a most useful book, *The Parish as a Learning Community*, he presents a helpful grid (1979, pp. 41–3). The graph for a learning congregation shows the directional as the base axis and the developing of relationships as the vertical, with collegial as the balancing of the two within which activity can take place (see Figure 9).

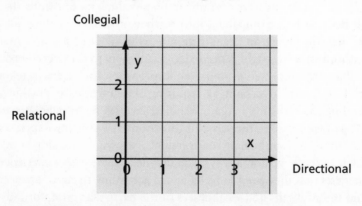

Figure 9 The learning congregation (Downs, 1979, pp. 41–3)

If there is oversensitivity regarding feelings and obtaining everyone's agreement, then little gets done. Alternatively, if plans and ideas are put into action in haste, people feel ignored or perhaps hurt. Experience has shown that consensus generously agreed and regular review of progress help to 'keep everyone on board' and allow growth, development and progress to continue. Personal growth and value and a sense of direction within congregations, achieved within boundaries of permission and agreement, can create health within a congregational grouping.

Leadership in church life

The word 'hierarchy' has its origin in church life (late Greek, *hierarchía* – rule or power of the high priest; Middle English, *jerarchie*; Middle French, *ierarchie*; Medieval Latin, *ierarchia*, variant of *hierarchia*). In church leadership it suggests an elevated and individualistic senior leadership with a rigid series of levels of authority 'below' it. An element of 'command and control' is almost implicit in structural understandings of hierarchy.

Stephen Pickard presents a different definition, giving the origin and meaning as 'sacred source': 'it is composed of two words – *hieros* meaning not priestly but sacred and *arche*, not rule but source or principle'. His view is that in ancient times it would have been assumed that the world was of divine origin, and this formed the basis for any understanding of it (Pickard, 2012, p. 162). As with the redefinition of *episkope* with released potential, here also is a reference to the nature of God which is discerned in ecclesiastical structures and which on occasions requires to be identified in emerging ways. In the life of our churches it is imperative to discern these faith or 'sacred source' characteristics.

Types and images of leader

Leaders are essential in any organization. Strong leaders are often wished for, but when they arrive their appointment may be regretted. When 'square pegs' are chosen, having the wrong person in place at the wrong time can cause years of difficulty for all concerned. At this stage in my exploration of oversight it is necessary to affirm the importance of the right leader for a particular stage in the development or drawing together of a group of parishes or congregations.

It is easy to caricature the style of any leader and we can be quick to complain when a leader, minister, vicar, chairperson or bishop demonstrates a different style from that wanted by a majority at a particular time. Problems arise for the person who finds themselves in what they perceive is the 'wrong job' just as much as for congregations who experience disappointment with a 'leader' who has been chosen after local consultation and involvement. In relation to multi-congregation situations, the needs of a wider series of communities have to be taken into account, since the person appointed to lead a team will be required to relate to many differing groups of people.

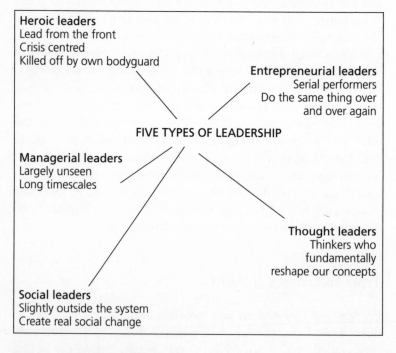

Figure 10 Personality and leadership

Figure 10 comes from work I have done with colleagues in leadership foundations associated with a range of professions in the UK. It has a particular relevance to the ways in which types of personality contribute to the effective development and working of multi-congregation groupings. It takes away the idea that 'one size fits all' and gives pointers to the type of leader and team required at a particular stage in a cycle.

The prevailing culture in the structures of church life, particularly but not exclusively in episcopal churches, remains leadership in an organized and graded hierarchy. However, the thrust of much organizational thinking leads to the idea that in the complexities of organizations and with the need for specialized knowledge in certain areas, the ability to work as a team is essential. Leaders have a particular role in the oversight of those who work with them as a team. This situation can present conflicting expectations within congregations, and requires exploration.

The heroic leader can be characterized as self-confident and will have a clear personal vision of what needs to be done to relieve a perceived crisis. In their experience, and sometimes aided by their inflated ego, oversimplified and personality-driven solutions will bring about a desired future. Such people have existed throughout history; sometimes they make history. The most talented appear to have an ability both to lead and to see a bigger picture which can be translated into interpreting a situation and mobilizing resources to overcome difficulty. In a grouping of local congregations an enormous leap needs to be made in identity, from individual self-contained congregations relating in a personal way to a minister to relating to a group of ministers and other 'partner' congregations. A leader driven by a strong concept of the value of these newly recognized groupings may contribute much from their own character and influence to the personality of what is established. Memories of this type of leader, many of whom will not actually see themselves as 'heroic', can last for decades or generations.

Entrepreneurial leaders see a good idea and want to develop it. They have an eye for opportunity and can build an organization around a new idea or product. They often operate in the voluntary and public sectors, while in churches they are good congregation-builders, social project developers, educators and trainers, as well as good preachers and communicators. They thrive in multi-congregation situations where the opportunities for them to use their skills are multiplied.

Such people have not only vision but also good leadership and managerial skills and are willing to take risks. A wide range of activities will be initiated, not all of which will last beyond the time the particular leader is in charge. Successful activities may become independent and be taken further by non-church community groups. The weakness in this leadership style is that entrepreneurs tend to repeat what they do over and over again. Once the vision and energy begin to wane, harking back to golden achievements in the past can be a characteristic and shows that freshness has gone.

Managerial leaders do not put themselves forward as heroes or saviours. They have long-term objectives and work away quietly and methodically at achieving them. They get things done through other people. Few will be remembered as remarkable but they are likely to achieve more than those who make a lot of noise and create much steam. At a certain stage in the life of a multi-congregation grouping such a leader will be just the right person. They may follow after a 'heroic' or entrepreneurial leader and establish or consolidate working systems which will deepen acceptance of new structures. Their failing may be to want to 'micro-manage' and not stay primarily with wider oversight responsibilities and roles.

One difficulty faced by managerial leaders when following a personality-focused leader is that congregation members may have a sense of personal loyalty to the departed leader which may override their loyalty to the present life and needs of the congregation. Since most systems and means of communication will have been routed through the heroic or entrepreneurial leader, it may be difficult to establish or consolidate functioning networks and structures.

Thought leaders are not the self-styled gurus who write popular 'how to' books with easy steps to achievement and clear analysis. Thought leaders rarely run organizations but develop theories and analysis which influence how we see the world, how we behave and how we understand ourselves. They may be best placed in assistant minister roles or as rural or area dean, directors of training or regional officers who work to bring into being and then support multi-congregation groupings. They will be good at vision and at suggesting the best theoretical structure for particular situations.

Social leaders are often either on the edges of mainstream activity or outside it completely. They show us another way. This type of leader will not just see alternative, sometimes counter-cultural, ways forward – they will create alternative organizations to demonstrate their ideas and vision of society. They will be driven by strong values and can communicate their vision effectively. They may be excited by forming new structures of just the kind needed as denominations move to larger groupings of congregations.

Leaders of multi-congregation groupings need to remain engaged with the wider community in which this church structure is set. Where congregations want to remain insular or turned in on themselves social leaders will feel a sense of isolation. The temptation will be to sit light to church activities and spend the majority of their time outside church structures finding colleagueship with other like-minded activists. Such leaders may introduce significant alternative ways for the local church to function, creating patterns and practices which will need a long timescale to become integral to the ways within which local ministries are understood.

Emerging oversight themes

Among those exercising an influence in current theological and ministerial circles is Stephen Pickard, an Australian academic and bishop who has worked for a time in the UK. In *Theological Foundations for Collaborative Ministry* he explores in some depth the foundations of ministerial writing in the nineteenth and early twentieth centuries. Of challenging significance for the study of contemporary interpretations of oversight is that alongside redefining hierarchy Pickard analyses the wording of Ordinals for the consecration of bishops. He concludes that the vows hardly match or describe the work to be done: 'it just might be possible that the vows are designed for a church that does not exist' (2009, p. 172). In a similar way, the words used in the licensing of a minister, particularly in the multi-congregation situations described above, also need to be rewritten with different emphases and revised local oversight tasks.

Of equal or perhaps greater significance is his 2012 book *Seeking the Church: An Introduction to Ecclesiology*. Pickard is concerned with the type of ecclesiology which he says 'attends to the *purpose* of the Church' (p. 7); examining the nature of Church, he sees it as 'the social outworking of faith with a direct relation to discerning the nature of the Kingdom of God' (p. 19). Important for my development later in this chapter, Pickard examines the variety of images used for the Church. He acknowledges that the 'models' proposed by Avery Dulles have had an enduring effect on how clergy and senior leaders understand their work (pp. 33–4).

The theologian Stephen Sykes has been an authority on Anglican identity and the nature of episcopal churches for three decades. In *Power and Christian Theology*, written after he had been a diocesan bishop, he argues that leaders should exercise judgement in a similar way to how a novelist develops a character through the circumstances of the story or 'plot' (Sykes, 2006). Sykes remains an important influence on the understanding of ministry and ecclesiology. His knowledge of German and Scandinavian theology has been an essential ingredient in ecumenical dialogue, and his images for oversight are referred to later in this chapter.

A helpful if provocative contribution about the nature of a church in the modern world is provided by the Aberdeen academic John Drane in what he describes as the 'McDonaldization' of the Church. He suggests that the essential content of Christianity has become so lost in modern methods of presentation that the essence did not satisfy those searching for a faith nor did it meet long-term evangelistic needs (Drane, 2000). In his later, more reflective book, *After McDonaldization*, Drane commends a Church which is more organic. He criticizes the current generation of church leaders who, rather than affirming the contribution of their pre-decessors, heap on them the blame for present problems and shortcomings. His view is that the churches concentrate too much on the 'heroic' leader at the expense of the image of 'servant' leader (2008, p. 103). His conclusion, however, is that Jesus was above all a 'relational' leader more than a servant leader (p. 117).

The works of Robin Greenwood, a ministerial theologian who has written about priesthood, ministry and church structure, have helped a generation of primarily non-evangelical clergy to reinterpret their ministry. In *Transforming Priesthood* (1994) his analysis of the malaise and often the anger of clergy in differ-ent parts of the developed world rings true. His establishment, or re-establishment, of the idea of the priest 'presiding' over the life and worship of a congregation has given a new focus for oversight ministries (p. 141). Much of his emphasis is on local ministry and the training schemes necessary for its development. His *Practising Community* (1996) and *The Ministry Team Handbook* (2000) mapped out emerging themes. He attempted to address some key inhibiting issues in *Transforming Church: Liberating Structures for Ministry* (2002), and identified the sense of powerlessness experienced by senior leaders in *Power: Changing Society and the Churches*, co-authored with Hugh Burgess (2005).

In *Parish Priests: For the Sake of the Kingdom* (2009) Green-wood takes the idea of oversight or *episkope* and interprets it as the presiding task of the local priest, acting as navigator and the person who relates the local church to its wider community. For

Greenwood *episkope* is a 'metaphor' which describes the task of the whole Church in relation to the world. He sees the leadership role of clergy as facilitators 'energizing' groups of congregations (p. 90). His Catholic emphasis is in the eucharistic community as the place where *episkope* is modelled.

Steven Croft writes from an evangelical perspective and has introduced many to the ecclesiastical language of leadership and oversight. His *Ministry in Three Dimensions* (1999) sets out a platform for Christian ministry for the ordained. It is described in three aspects – diaconal, presbyteral and episcopal. His contribution has been to give a theological framework for the church growth movement, in particular in Anglican form. The aim is to create missionary congregations with clergy motivating the laity. His point about the early Church choosing its own language, not borrowing from the secular, is interesting for those involved in the study of church leadership; it could be challenged since each of these words were in secular use at the time of the emergence of the first Christian communities. The important development relating to leadership is in the section on *episkope*, where the role of the leader is stated as 'to watch over the congregation, guarding its unity' (p. 154) and 'to enable the ministry of others' (p. 166). His development of the minister as someone who needs to watch over and care for themselves is developed in his later FCL booklet *Focus on Leadership* and has been influential for senior leaders and parish clergy alike (2005).

Monica Furlong has produced one of the most comprehensive and critical studies of the changes taking place in the Church of England, which is also of significance as it comments from a female perspective on a predominantly male-governed Church. In Part Two of her book *The C of E: The State It's In* (2000), she is severely critical of its centralizing tendencies. Furlong, alongside Peter Selby, introduces the concept of 'tribalism' in a male-dominated Church and the 'family secret' about the unwillingness to accept and discuss in public some of the Church's major failings (p. 253).

Thompson and Thompson do not like the origins of the word *episkope*, with its associations with the 'taskmasters' who oversaw the work of Hebrew slaves in Egypt. They back away from the significant and important internalization of the implications of a renewed understanding of oversight, instead preferring the weaker 'overview' (Thompson and Thompson, 2012, p. 93). Cocksworth and Brown attempt to enter into the nature of vocation in a changing, adapting and developing Church of England. In *Being a Priest Today* (2002) they examine whether priestly ministry is functional or ontological. Their metaphor is of 'the vine', describing priestly connectedness to both Christ and the people served as 'relational'; it is 'the sap' which brings energy to ministry.

John Pritchard, formerly Bishop of Oxford, has tried an approach which uses mind pictures, active images rather than models, to describe the work of the priest or minister today. He structured his book *The Life and Work of a Priest* (2007) using a long series of descriptive phrases: spiritual explorer, artful storyteller, pain-bearer, wounded companion, iconic presence, faith-coach and flower arranger. Pritchard's writing is well researched and in an accessible style. It has found a resonance with both parish clergy and laypeople. Keith Lamdin, Principal of Sarum College, in a book based on his wide training experience, attempts to enable clergy to 'find their leadership style' using images such as monarch, warrior, servant, prophet, contemplative and elder (Lamdin, 2012).

European theologians in the Roman Catholic Church have been a significant influence in proposing how oversight and collegiality could be experienced among church leaders. One of the most significant contemporary public critics of leadership in the Catholic Church is the Tübingen theologian Hans Küng. His position is an attempt to obtain greater collegiality in decision-making, which he holds was the intention of the Second Vatican Council and has since been subject to a systematic process of erosion.

In all this, the collegiality of church government which the Council 'in theory' fought for, in other words the collegial responsibility of Pope and Bishops for the whole church, is criminally ignored and passed over. This shared responsibility, grounded in Bible and tradition, called for by the present situation and affirmed by the Council by 1808 votes to 336, may have been celebrated as a great victory for the Council, but the Curia goes on working after the Council as if collegiality had never been decided on. (Küng, 2008, p. 23)

Küng's major writings about the nature of the whole Church, and its existence in relation to the present and developing Roman Catholic Church, are an enduring legacy. He feels that the 'spirit' of the Second Vatican Council was not carried forward either by subsequent papal appointments or by the centralized Vatican bureaucracy which was charged with this task. His two-volume autobiography charts his hopes and frustrations while choosing to remain a priest within the Catholic Church. It also describes his later emphases on world development and ecology (Küng, 2008).

In looking at the presence and work of a priest in a Christian community and beyond in *Why Priests?*, Küng says:

A good church leader can *inspire*, *moderate* and *animate* a community. They will not imagine they are the Holy Spirit, but realize that their own flesh is weak and that they do not need to be a genius or an exemplary saint ... A good church leader is also one who proclaims the word in their community with authority. (Küng, 1972, p. 88)

The Dutch Catholic theologian Edward Schillebeeckx has attracted much attention, including investigation from the Vatican, particularly for his writings on ministry. His *Ministry: A Case for Change* (1981) and *The Church with a Human Face* (1985) map developments in ministries within the Church over two millennia. He concludes that from early relational beginnings, together with a strong sense of ownership, from the fourth century onwards the Church developed taking civil parallels first from the Roman Empire and later through what he calls a 'feudal spirituality' (1985, pp. 147–65). He argues for a radically adapted Church formed by 'listening to the complaints of the people' (pp. 209–36) and especially by listening to the 'discontent among women' (pp. 236–40). His reconstruction includes adaptation of the absolute rule of celibacy for secular clergy (pp. 240–54).

Taking an associated approach is Jürgen Moltmann, a theologian from the European Reformed Churches. In *The Crucified
God* (1974) he examines and proposes with revealing honesty the
overseeing relationship of God to suffering people. Most significant for this research is *The Church in the Power of the Spirit*
(1977). In this important and formative book he analyses the
development of ministries within the Church in a similar way to
Küng, and in an associated but distinctively different way from
Schillebeeckx in that he sees developments in ministry, and their
adaptation through history, as driven by the influence and energy
derived from the Holy Spirit. He develops these ideas as forming and re-forming the 'character' of a Christian community in
The Open Church: Invitation to a Messianic Lifestyle (1978). It
is interesting to observe the number of writers drawn into this
discussion of oversight, Schillebeeckx and Adair included, who
refer on a number of occasions to the fact that the Church is in a
constant process of forming and re-forming itself.

Researchers of leadership and oversight

The University of Cambridge recently brought to a close a project
to examine the relationship between psychology and religion. The
Psychology and Religion Research Group (PRRG) was formed
shortly after Fraser Watts took up his appointment as Starbridge
Lecturer in Theology and Natural Science in the university in
1994. Building upon his long and fruitful career in the human
sciences, Watts turned his attention to developing the collaborative
possibilities between psychology and religion. Two related publications have been produced: *Psychology for Christian Ministry*
by Watts et al. (2002) and *The Human Face of the Church* by
Sara Savage and Eolene Boyd-Macmillan (2007). These combine
significant pieces of research with accessible writing and explore
the organizational make-up of congregations, their clergy and
their religious leaders.

Richard Roberts, based now in the University of Lancaster, is
particularly concerned with organizations becoming operational

in a bureaucratic and mechanized way. Considering his experience of the Church of Scotland and that of the Church of England, he makes strident and critical comments about the direction both churches have travelled (Roberts, 2002). Using the work of Troeltsch and later of Sykes he argues that the initial energy and 'power' which the Spirit gave to churches was subsumed by the creation of hierarchies which gradually took power to themselves in ways which stifled individualism and prevented initiative. He goes on to group modern episcopal churches with other institutions which in post-war years exhibit signs of what he calls 'the end of history': the loss of shared human universals, 'culture wars' and the end of an 'age of ideology' (p. 2). He says that churches following suit are now characterized by the kind of 'managerialism' proposed in the Church of England's Turnbull Report, *Working as One Body* (1995). He concludes, in his most critical chapter of the way the Church of England has developed: 'In the *uncritical* assimilation of managerialism the Church of England has, in Havel's terms, been seduced by the reality and promise of power restored over a subject "other", a pattern all too tempting in a managerial society' (p. 188).

The first person to attempt to introduce what were then thought of as management rather than leadership concepts in the Anglican and Roman Catholic Churches and the religious orders was Peter Rudge. With an initial training in economics and business administration, Rudge brought an objective critique to church life. From 1970 onwards his consultancy work with CORAT (Christian Organizations, Research and Advisory Trust) provided guidance for how clergy could be prepared for oversight roles. *Management in the Church* set out his work in a systematic way (1976). He has compared religious and secular organizations, outlining some of the differences in church life – length in office, security of tenure and extremely long working hours – which presented specific managerial contexts.

Attempting to give perspective to the many schools within the sociology of organizations Rudge developed a typology grid describing and analysing the principal leadership types and their proponents. In *Order and Disorder in Organizations*, to Weber's traditional, charismatic and bureaucratic types Rudge adds classical (running a machine), human-relations (leading groups) and systemic (adapting a system) (Rudge, 1990, pp. 38–57, 156–75, chart pp. 160–3). Most interesting is the way in which Rudge examines the various 'discourses' organizational writers use and the language and metaphors within them. He uses 'spread sheet' tabulation of leadership styles and compares them with images of the Church, mainly from the Bible, and comes to an interesting conclusion:

> In the Millett and Lake Chart they are saying that there are no Biblical images of the church which reflect or support a conception of the church in mechanistic terms. They say the imposition of mechanical models assumes that certain areas of church life are better organized without God as personal ... It follows, therefore, that any introduction of mechanistic concepts or phrases into theological discourse about church do not have a counterpart in Biblical theology. (Rudge, 1990, p. 166)

That said, the work of many ministerial theologians has included a rich range of ideas and experience which when taken together do suggest that there are helpful groupings of ideas which give a framework for the exercise of oversight.

Core components of oversight

It is now possible to take the metaphors, concepts, leadership styles and mind pictures described so far and place them in a new structure to provide a framework which will help to nurture identity and create and sustain the work of oversight. This will be done through identifying aspects and understandings of leadership and oversight from previous chapters, and grouping them together so that they interrelate to form core aspects for effective oversight. This method requires a 'health warning', since the identification and naming of exclusive concepts for leadership can be restricting and not allow for wider interpretation. To 'trap' a leader in one received 'caricature' can be enormously damaging to the effectiveness of their work. It can even threaten the more comprehensive and varied understandings of leadership which are necessary for any organization if it is to develop and change.

In his foundational and influential study, *Images of Organization: Of the Nature of Metaphor and its Importance in Organization and Management*, Gareth Morgan has examined the use of 'models' derived from metaphor and imagery in ways which can both shape thinking and warn against overdependence:

> Metaphor is inherently paradoxical. It can create powerful insights that also become distortions, as the way of seeing through a metaphor becomes a way of *not* seeing. (Morgan, 1997, p. 5)

Metaphor is a figure of speech in which we speak about one thing in terms that are usually employed to describe something else. Metaphors work by drawing our attention to certain features of things, while simultaneously screening other aspects from our attention. Morgan says, 'Metaphors create ways of seeing and shaping organizational life ... Different metaphors have a capacity to tap different dimensions of a situation, showing how different qualities can co-exist.' It will become clear that images cannot be 'contained', and many could sit with some comfort in another of my categories. Given the importance of metaphor within religious texts it is only a logical development that these categories can be employed to shed light on the nature of the religious language of oversight. Grouping models into 'families', as with Adair's task, team and individual, and Stamp's tasking, tending and trusting, can give a range and sophistication to interpretations of a type or style of leadership.

Wesley Carr has been a significant influence on generations of church leaders. His analytical writing and informed consultancy have deepened ministerial understandings of work for clergy at all levels of responsibility. In *The Priestlike Task* he commends the use of models in attempting to understand ministry within the churches:

The term 'model' is widely used today ... A model of ministry, therefore, which is founded upon the day-to-day experience of the church may both provide coherence and prompt persistent review and systematic scrutiny. Out of this will come new approaches to problems, possibly new patterns of ministry, and, with the continual re-evaluation of the model itself, managed change. (Carr, 1985, p. 13)

The theologian Avery Dulles explored the concept of a particular kind of modelling. In his *Models of the Church* (1974) he described the Church as institution, mystical communion, sacrament, herald, and servant. Writing from a Roman Catholic point of view his 'mind picture' method of ecclesiological modelling caught the imagination of the times. In this analysis he gave voice to what clergy and bishops wanted to express as the shape of their work but had not until then found the vocational and conceptual language.

The method of modelling used by Avery Dulles was criticized by another Roman Catholic writer and academic, Thomas Downs, Director of Education in the Diocese of Orlando in the late 1970s and early 1980s. In *The Parish as a Learning Community* (1979) he distinguished between what he calls 'theoretical' and 'experimental' models (pp. 15–23). He analysed the models described by Dulles as being what he called theoretical – 'holistic, describing the whole rather than the parts'. By this he meant that such models were descriptive and static. He contrasted this with experimental models which were more descriptive, 'describing the trees as well as the wood'. Downs also comments on the contrast between Church as an institution and Church as a community (pp. 15–16). The dynamic nature of these models or concepts will be emphasized in the construction of proposals from the lived experience of local churches and the reflective experience of ministerial theologians.

Theological modelling for effective oversight

One of the difficulties in taking what are disparagingly called 'managerial models' and applying them to church life is that it can provoke a hostile response. For this reason, the essential import- ance of theology in understanding how organizations work has been emphasized. It is now possible to group the words, images, metaphors and general descriptions used by church leaders, from the Bible onwards, for their work. The examples are many and individual leaders make much of their own selected models or images to develop and sustain their own ministries.

Some biblical images

Any list has to begin with images and descriptions of God and of Jesus as teacher. This image begins with the mind picture from Judaism of Jesus as a rabbi who teaches by listening and engages his followers through the use of imagery, story and picture language. St John develops the sayings about the sheep knowing and being known by their shepherd, hearing and trust- ing his voice, and of Jesus being the gate of the sheepfold; varying the analogy, Jesus is created as the 'good shepherd' (John 10). In the Old Testament are found references to God as **shepherd**, the most familiar of these being in Psalm 23. Other instances occur at Genesis 49.24, Psalm 80.1 and Ecclesiastes 12.11. Among the many images and descriptions of God and Jesus, those of **teacher**, **listener** and **shepherd** emerge.

In his own ministry it is clear that Jesus chose the image of ser- vant for himself. He took this from the so-called 'servant songs' in the book of the prophet Isaiah and it is among the clearest pointers to his own formation and to the underlying values which motivated him, especially when under pressure (Isa. 49–53). This image has been taken up widely, and in modern secular terms principally by the description of servant leadership by Robert Greenleaf and the Greenleaf Foundation (www.greenleaf.org).

St Paul is the great systematizer of the early Christian faith. In his letters he can be observed wrestling to make sense of this new faith in relation to his previous training and as a guide to emerging Christian communities. Like a chef, he arranges and rearranges ingredients as he develops his thinking in relation to the new congregations he is writing to. Paul makes much of the sacrificial servant theme in his teaching and guidance to the early Church. He insists that the significance of Christ's death on the cross is that he paid a price and delivered freedom from slavery for all who believe in him (1 Cor. 6.20, 7.23). Believers are no longer slaves but children of God (Gal. 4.7). This comes with a warning, especially for leaders, that they should not become slaves to others (1 Cor. 7.23). His letter to the Romans is one of the great achievements of the 'chef' arranging and detailing ingredients. Theologians and reformers from St Augustine of Hippo to Martin Luther, John Calvin, John Wesley and Karl Barth have used the same mixing and transforming methodology to develop systematic theology for their age and to address particular social and cultural situations. Among the images used by these formative characters we can identify **chef**, **servant**, **slave** and **child**.

Images from history and tradition

In identifying images and metaphors from the uses and descriptions of oversight an array of 'mind pictures' emerge. All are relevant to the work and roles of those engaged in understanding and developing work in multi-congregation ministries. The potential is so great that only selective examples can be taken, at the risk of being exclusive or superficial. Prophets saw themselves as interpreters and on occasion heralds of new and changing times, taking on a liminal role in their public utterances. In the Bible a scapegoat was a goat that was driven off into the wilderness as part of the ceremonies of Yom Kippur, the Day of Atonement, in Judaism during the times of the Temple in Jerusalem. The ritual is described in Leviticus 16, where the goat, with the sins of the people placed on it, is sent away to perish. In an interesting variation Savage and Boyd-Macmillan explore modern scapegoats: how the insecure or monarchical leader will target more able team or staff members, people they see as a threat (2007, p. 12). Jesus himself was influenced in a significant way by Isaiah's image of **servant**. St John in particular developed this imagery of the 'suffering servant' taking on themselves the responsibility for the misdeeds of others as he reordered the trial and crucifixion narrative in his Gospel (John 18, 19). It was Gregory the Great who first applied the image of the 'servant of the servants' to the episcopal leader. It is possible to begin from such sources to build a series of images which include **scapegoat, servant, herald** and **monarch**.

Church leaders and their metaphors

Archbishop John Sentamu said that in his own original language a leader is defined as 'pioneer', and also someone 'who clears the forest and makes a path'. Sentamu, Greenwood and Küng all use the term 'bridge-builder'. Bishop Peter Price has spoken of the need for the leader to be a 'map-maker'. From his work in New Zealand Robin Greenwood has developed the concept of the leader as navigator. It was, as we have seen, Gregory the Great who applied the biblical image of the servant to the role of a Christian leader. In sending emissaries out to convert pagan nations Augustine gives the bishop leader the role of missioner or strategist. Reflecting on the work of a bishop just before his retirement in summer 2009, Kenneth Stevenson chose 'speaker' – as in Speaker of the House of Commons – as one model which described the work of a diocesan bishop, chair or president. He saw himself as the 'rogue' leader, one who has an uneasy relationship with their organization. So in the construction of my long list the following images can be identified: **pioneer, bridge-builder, map-maker, navigator, missioner, strategist, speaker, monarch, chairman** and **rogue**.

It is significant that a new generation of theologians of ministry have chosen models or creative imagery to describe the work of clergy. In this they are developing the work of Dulles, who described the Church as institution, mystical communion, sacrament, herald and servant, and giving each practical application.

Contemporary writers who come closest to using *episkope* as a model include Thompson and Thompson (2012, pp. 92–6). They identify four leadership styles: **overview, administrative servant, visionary** and **enabler**.

Savage and Boyd-Macmillan begin their analysis of what encourages growth in faith by what they call a cheeky use of a famous statement by Chairman Mao: 'Let a thousand flowers bloom' – introducing the organic concept of gardener (2007, p. 183). Stephen Sykes takes the advice given by Gregory the Great and examines the tantalizing balance between being an authority figure and, by teaching and example, enabling others to grow (2006, pp. 139–41). The leader is a kind of authority figure and this can be understood in various ways through imagery and metaphor. Aspects of dependency and independency have been explored extensively and innovatively by the Grubb Institute, primarily through the writings of its founding director Bruce Reed. His 'oscillation theory', worked out in the seminal book *The Dynamics of Religion*, has taken this thinking of the place of parent or guardian figure to interesting and challenging places (Reed, 1978).

The leader or leadership team, has to reprimand and discipline as well as encourage. Most would admit that this role does not sit comfortably with that of pastor, and it can eat into a disproportionate amount of their time. Sykes develops the parallels of responsibility between bishops and other senior leaders in his study of power (Sykes, 2006, p. 137). The role of those in power, such as a prime minister, is partly to 'guard' the nation and to defend it against attack. Sykes outlines the responsibilities for the work of bishop as being similar to a chief overseer. Stephen Cherry has developed the theme of the need for humility in order to be a listener with 'passionate humility' in effective ways (Cherry, 2011). Here is a development of relational, listening images and models arising from **body** and **heartbeat, parent, guardian, disciplinarian** and **listener**.

Component concepts for oversight

The wide range of description, metaphor and mind pictures identified up to this point can be grouped into 'families' or concepts,
leading to the identification of three fundamental characteristics
or requirements in the exercise of oversight. They develop the
concept of Peter Senge's fifth discipline of systems thinking, where
it is the integration of ideas, concepts and mental models into
a systematic order which provides the energy and structure for
overview. The local leader needs to understand their own role,
discern needs, evaluate resources, make strategic appointments,
and nurture and guide in a disciplined and authoritative way.

The first task is to list the images and metaphors identified
above to create a long list. This list can then suggest the creation
of embryonic categories. The following have been identified:
**teacher, listener, shepherd, chef, servant, slave, child, pioneer,
bridge-builder, map-maker, navigator, reformer, strategist,
speaker, monarch, rogue, herald, servant, gardener, scapegoat,
parent, guardian, disciplinarian** and **listener**. From earlier chapters other roles can be added: **lawyer, legitimator** and exemplar
of holiness (**saint**). The list could be extended yet further since the
description of religious activity and faith depends to some degree
on the use of metaphor and analogy.

The second task is to describe and explore this imagery in
categories which cover particular areas of role or responsibility.
Three groupings can be identified which incorporate images from
the list above. Although to some extent they develop the initial
categories identified by Adair, Stamp and Downs, in another
sense the overarching categories are distinctive and arise from an
overview of the research carried out so far and a reasoned sense
of how images can be grouped. They reflect the need for members
of any organization to feel that they are encouraged and allowed
to grow and develop wherever they find themselves. The first
category is **organic**. The second describes the need for people to
feel that there is a sense of purpose rather than drift or stagnation
in their organization, and this category is **directional**. The third
expresses the need for guardianship of tradition, for boundaries

to be established and managed, and discipline to be administered – by leaders who command respect, and this category is **authoritative**.

The third task, then, is to describe the development of these new categories of oversight from those already identified as having lasting significance in the practice of organizational and role analysis. The generic compilation groupings of **organic**, **directional** and **authoritative** give the 'synoptic' view which is the essential ingredient for the effective exercise of oversight in multi-congregation ministries, and in other devolved organizations (see Figure 11).

Adair	Individual	Task	Team
Stamp	Tending	Tasking	Trusting
Downs	Relational	Directional	Collegial
Grundy	*Organic*	*Directional*	*Authoritative*

Figure 11 Proposing an oversight grid

These generic headings or concepts, drawn from whatever range of sources, are what congregation members are looking for in the ministers called by their church to provide oversight and leadership. For the ministers, a grasp of the essential characteristics and privileges of the work gives coherence to what can seem like disparate situations in which competing demands press on them every day. Whatever individual leadership style is adopted, the responsibilities of oversight remain the same, although they will be interpreted in different ways according to personality and the range of situations.

Without these essential and integrated components integrity will be lacking and trust not established and maintained. Identifying a balance of integrated concepts brings together the need for *episkope* or oversight to be expressed in a clear and memorable way. Ecumenical expressions of *episkope* can be understood within the ecclesial community as arising from its common life, deriving from the apostolic nature of oversight contained within the universal Church, and examined within the ecumenical agreements of the past 50 years. When integrated with current ministerial practice and writings, these provide words and concepts in common everyday use. They arise from theological sources and reflect the nature of the divine Creator God. Drawing on the work of ministerial theologians and practitioners as well as on organizational thinkers has achieved this.

Organic	Directional	Authoritative
Enabler	Shepherd	Parent/Guardian
Gardener	Map-maker	Reformer
Chef	Navigator	Lawyer
Servant	Bridge-builder	Legitimator
Scapegoat	Missioner	Prime Minister
Speaker	Rogue	Monarch
Teacher	Interpreter	Prefect
Listener	Pioneer	Listener
Child	Strategist	Slave
Saint	Herald	Discipliner
(the list could be extended/contested)		

Figure 12 Sources for an oversight grid

The generic grid for the responsibilities of local oversight (see Figure 12) can be further simplified and summarized. It represents the requirements of the exercise of *episkope* expressed as oversight in a devolved organization. It describes the synoptic overview needed to give vision, provide influence and exercise pastoral care, often at a distance and frequently through other people. The three fundamental aspects for effective oversight are not mutually exclusive and the ideal exercise of oversight at any level would reflect an understanding that each of the three categories need to be present and integrated in any healthy organization or Church (see Figure 13).

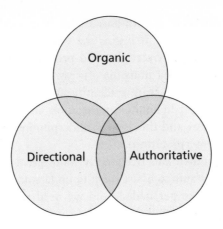

Figure 13 Balanced theological modelling for effective oversight

From theory to practice

Local groupings of congregations often produce material and courses to assist congregations to get to know one another. This kind of activity is essential before evangelistic or faith development programmes are begun. Joint services, combined social activities, pilgrimages and socializing, may all be necessary before trust and deeper sharing can be achieved.

It can only be a matter of time before examples of good practice are published. Already the Church Pastoral Aid Society (CPAS) is developing material for multi-benefice ministries. Robin Greenwood, who has contributed much to our understanding of congregational and ministerial practice, is developing work through the William Leach Foundation. His intention is to enable structured conversations to take place within and between congregations.

Such research and writing are all aimed at supporting change through time. No doubt the pitfalls and challenges will be described, along with the successes, as new patterns of ministry become consolidated. By linking theology and practice in this chapter it has been my intention to move through the experience and comment of leaders to establish a faith-based way of understanding the nature of local oversight. It begins the work of reinterpreting a 'calling' to this kind of oversight, and provides an escape route from being overcome by immediate pressures suggesting spaces where Keith Elford's nurturing identity and creating the future can fit in. Oversight in multi-congregation situations needs its own interpretations and theological underpinning. It demands a new vocational interpretation.

Teams and individuals frequently find great benefit from employing consultants to assist them in understanding their role. Others remain to be persuaded, and we need to explore which personal and organizational support resources can be of most assistance for the development of effective ministries of oversight. This is examined in the next chapter in order to demonstrate how such resources to support a vocation to quite new kinds of ministerial work can be embraced and utilized to best advantage.

5

Watching Over with Integrity

One of the most difficult aspects of oversight is the ability to maintain personal integrity while living with the pressures and expectations imposed by others. No aspect of leadership is straightforward and with personal gratification may come the temptation to separate oneself from the support and colleague-ship of others. Analysis of leadership styles and the fundamental needs of those in congregations has produced a richness of under-standing and a multiplicity of resources. My descriptions of the essential characteristics of oversight as organic, directional and authoritative give an outline of what congregations need, and also a 'job description' of responsibility for those called to ministries of oversight. There is now a need to establish and describe the essentials of formation and support for ministries of oversight in multi-congregation and other congregational settings.

In the Preface I remarked that I have watched colleagues take on further responsibilities and seen that the culture and the pressures of their work have turned them into different people – and not always for the better! That is why it is important to give a whole chapter to the development or construction of a 'support system' for those called to particular oversight responsibilities. I referred in Chapter 1 to Martyn Percy's view that those charged with the responsibility for oversight need to understand how those 'under' them learn. He makes an important point also about how we all learn some things from those with responsibility to watch over us:

Often, we learn from those in oversight who are able to display character and virtue, not just skill; enormous reserves of resilience, patience and energy. In which insight and courage are fused to gentle but firm will. (Percy, 2013, p. 15)

I now want to explore how that 'character and virtue' are formed and sustained, both for those who have the responsibility for oversight and for those who work with them and learn from them.

Much of what is outlined here is applicable across denominations and also to non-church organizations. Clearly the language would need to be amended and the evidence base broadened but the lessons, responsibilities, temptations and pitfalls remain the same. That some of the concepts underlying this study are taken from secular leadership theorists reinforces this point of view. Essential to any parallels which are drawn is the way in which churches are understood as being composed of many local congregations, in the same way as large companies may be composed of many local units – factories, offices or shops.

An extension of the oversight model constructed in Chapter 4 provides a frame of reference within which this much-needed support can be constructed, allowing people to understand the approaches they bring to their work. Work consultancy resources and the contribution of writers and commentators come into play here. According to David Dadswell, if there were not coherence or 'joined-up' thinking about the range of resources available the consultant or educator would continue to use a 'smorgasbord' approach, picking and choosing practical and theoretical models at will. He advocates a disciplined alternative:

> Consultants will only be of use to the consultor if they can integrate a range of disciplines. It may be necessary to draw on theology, biblical studies, ecclesiology, missiology, sociology, organizational studies, congregational studies, psychology, group dynamics, management and anthropology, to name a few. A gifted consultant will be able to handle a relevant, healthy interaction of disciplines. (Dadswell, 2011, p. xiii)

The many elements which contribute to a wider understanding of oversight need to be brought together to provide a 'healthy interaction of disciplines', and this can be achieved by transforming my 'flat' grid or groupings of models so that they generate four multi-dimensional 'faces'. If done effectively, this will provide the dynamic impetus for a range of disciplines. Essential elements in any understanding of oversight need to take into account a number of factors:

- the pressures and influences of public ministry
- the places where experience is gained
- the need for continuing personal development
- the dangers which come with the prolonged responsibility.

The establishment of 'faces' in a developed oversight grid provides the opportunity not otherwise achievable to integrate a wide range of spirituality and skills training resources. Ministers exercising oversight, practitioners and trainers, as well as those who reflect in a theological way about the responsibilities of leadership and oversight, may find it provocative, stimulating and useful. This four-faced diagram takes a 'one-dimensional' concept and gives it layer upon layer of depth (see Figure 14).

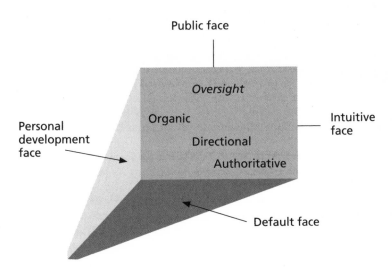

Figure 14 The four dynamic faces of oversight

The necessary establishment and expansion of these dynamic concepts is discussed in the following sections. Under each main heading or 'face' a series of subsections follow which draw on the experience and writing of colleagues and theologians. The aim is to do more than expand a concept, and try to produce integrated thinking and support.

Leaders are always in the public gaze, so there is the **public** face of oversight. Such responsibility requires making decisions observed by colleagues, employees and volunteers, among others. Competing pressures and demands have to be balanced in decision-making. Listening to and understanding others are essential skills. Credible leadership requires the ability to articulate a vision and embody the values of the institution.

Experience of leadership over some length of time enables the development of an **intuitive** face. This involves being able to see beyond the evidence to new possibilities and directions. Complexity has to be managed and this requires the leader to be reflective, to critique prevalent and emerging models, and to accompany and guide to new places.

The self-aware minister or church leader is always concerned with the **personal development** face of their life and work. For Christians or faith leaders this requires a constant relating of faith to practice and to the demands of the job. Many leaders use psychological profiling as a means of personal understanding. Researchers use psychometric tests to analyse and describe leadership paths and styles. Church leaders may use secular rather than religious training agencies to help them reflect on their experience and to interpret their behaviour and that of members of their work groups.

Under pressure there may be the temptation to revert to a **default position** face which sometimes surprises leaders and those they work with. On occasion they may wonder who they really are and who they are becoming as a result of the job. The self-aware are conscious of how they can make difficult decisions and still retain their integrity. Others are less aware, and may show a tendency towards self-aggrandizement or hubris as a consequence of long-term leadership.

Thus the expansion of my oversight model with its three essential characteristics reinforces the practical evidence which formed the original concept of modelling. Oversight requires certain personal and organizational skills which can lead to greater self-understanding and give the opportunity for objective measurement for review, training and evaluation.

The public face of oversight

Every leader is exposed to public scrutiny of one kind or another. In the local church, and the rural churches especially, an awareness of where the minister is across multi-congregation groupings is carried by the local 'grapevine'. It is essential that support mechanisms are in place which can enable a leader to operate in the heat of the moment and to make decisions and pronouncements which are understood (even if not affirmed) by team and congregation members. Leaders need to know how to prepare themselves for such challenging situations. Decisions need to be made within the overall context of oversight.

Public face
Use leadership moments
Balance competing demands
Listen and understand
Articulate a vision
Embody the values of the institution
Learn to ensure communication

Figure 15 The public face of oversight

Use leadership moments

People who take on leadership responsibility at any level often speak of how aware they are of being in the public eye and the pressure they are under to make immediate decisions. Some say that the decision-making begins on the day they accept the post, and certainly from the day of its announcement. This can be the experience of anyone taking on expanded responsibilities in grouped local congregations. The processes which have formed the newly appointed leader and the experience they have gained in various ways are immediately put to the test.

The need to make instant decisions with little time to reflect is described and analysed by Chris Blakely and Sue Howard in their Grove booklet, *The Inner Life of a Christian Leader* (2010). Interestingly they note that as well as clear situations when a decision has to be made, at many other times decisions can be communicated by silence or by body language. They say that particularly significant are not the 'either-or' types of decision, but those which come in the form of a question which makes those who want someone else to make a decision see their request or dilemma in a completely different way. This was the rabbinical way and the method used frequently by Jesus himself (p. 14).

Replying with another question will not always be well received, and indeed will sometimes be avoiding the responsibility of shepherding which is a part of oversight. Alternatively, what is sometimes called 'appreciative enquiry' will produce more deeply remembered and acted-on results. Blakely and Howard make particularly interesting points on this subject and suggest that a key element in the accumulated experience of a leader is the ability to discern the 'leadership moment': when it is appropriate and necessary to be decisive, and when it is not. They call this the *kairos* moment – the significant time when an action, gesture or decision is needed which will affect the long-term future of a person or organization (p. 14). The building up of experience, supported by consultancy and reflection, will make these moments more timely and effective.

Balance competing demands

For the busy leader, the difficulty of finding time to discern which action is needed and the awareness of competing demands can cause stress, provoke inappropriate behaviour under pressure, and bring about the type of decision which seems to give preference to one group or the interests of a particular individual. John Adair's Venn diagram provides a template for thought where the identification of task, team and individual become important. Adair gives a warning about a less than critical use of his template:

> It follows that your relationship with each individual in your team will be different. For each person will evoke a fact of your own personality. Like a parent, however, you should ensure that these relationships are essentially professional, not to be confused with friendships. For friendships grow from liking some people more than others, which has the corollary that you like others less. And people, not being short on discernment, will soon see where your personal preferences lie. (Adair, 2002, p. 241)

Balancing competing demands is at the core of the practice of oversight and remains an inevitable pressure on the individual leader. As this can never be achieved to the satisfaction of equally competing groups and individuals, an inner confidence is needed and resources are available to enable demands to be met with equanimity and a sense of fairness.

Listen and understand

The inclusion of listening as part of the necessary make-up and formation of a leader identifies an essential skill and training need. Christopher Edmondson's work on how leaders need to listen has become influential (Edmondson, 2010). His examination of the barriers to good communication is perceptive. Whether, as Edmondson suggests, good listening can lead to prophetic interpretation remains open to challenge. Stephen Covey presents seven habits of highly effective people, and the first three are about the need to learn to listen. He develops the concept of 'emphatic listening', the idea that the leader has to 'feel' as well as hear what is being said (Covey, 1989, pp. 239–43).

During my time at the Foundation for Church Leadership we commissioned Eolene Boyd-Macmillan and Sara Savage from the Psychology of Religion Research group of the Faculty of Divinity at Cambridge University to develop a research project on Conflict Transformation. An essential element of this was an understanding of multi-layered listening – 'to ourselves and to others' (Boyd-Macmillan and Savage, 2008). This programme was initially offered to 29 church leaders and became a formative piece of reflective training. Regarding the need for leaders to listen and for groups to listen to one another, Boyd-Macmillan and Savage say: 'Half the messiness of conflict arises from both "sides" not feeling "heard"' (p. 72).

Articulate a vision

Following immediately from the requirement to listen is the need to express what is being seen and heard. One great privilege of oversight is that the leader can be enabled to 'see a bigger picture' than those committed to work in local situations. The truism (and a valuable biblical proverb) that 'without vision the people perish' reinforces my directional aspect of the essentials of oversight (Prov. 29.18).

The reflective listener with an ability to clarify questions and see to the heart of problems has much to offer and will be given an authoritative hearing. Using the language of the Christian leader Tony McCaffry describes this well:

> The church leader with the God-view aspiration does not impose pre-set responses to problems: such fundamentalism, providing the answer to the question yet to be raised, gives little respect to the individuality of the Christ-bearer other who, like the leader, is a learner whose integrity is to be respected. This does not rule out the leader's prophetic role as the signpost pointing the way of the Lord to the pilgrim traveller. (McCaffry, 2008, p. 358)

Embody the values of the institution

Emphatic listening is not all a leader is expected to do. Part of the task of oversight is to measure what is being said and hoped for against the history, traditions and values of the organization. According to Michael Ramsey, one of the earliest reasons for the appointment of trusted and authoritative local *episkopoi* to 'oversee' the local churches was to guard and embody the tradition (Ramsey, 1936). Similarly it was the Council of Nicea in 325 which decided on the need for one respected and authoritative bishop to have 'oversight' over a number of dioceses and be called 'metropolitan' or, in effect, 'archbishop'.

The work of a church leader is always set in the context of the church they 'lead'. Turnbull and McFadyen assert that 'the nature of required leadership cannot be determined without an understanding of the organization which they are appointed to lead' (2012, p. 110). This is a two-way road. Nurture is needed to ensure that a leader is formed by the traditions and spirituality of their denomination while at the same time confidence is required to develop these values as challenges to the way things are now. The question remains, *Quis custodiet ipsos custodes?* ('Who guards the guards?').

Learn to ensure communication

Communication is about more than the ability to appear in public and speak fluently, explaining decisions which have been or need to be taken. Communication is about understanding how decisions move through an organization, and assisting and enabling that movement. The appropriate and sensitive release of information is a vital ingredient which applies to many aspects of oversight. The ability to withhold the outcome of a decision or related information may mean that one person or group knows more than another.

In this study, where the concept of oversight defined as to 'watch over one another in community' is a primary consideration, the experience of poor communication is serious indeed. Adair makes the fundamental point that communication is essential at as many levels as possible:

> A good time manager ... also has time to communicate to the whole organization. Both personal and direct, this communication extends beyond the upper crust of management, and touches as many people as possible. The aim is to align the critical mass of the operational and team leaders, and ultimately everyone, with the broad strategic direction. This in turn will inform goals and the setting of objectives in all parts of the organization. (Adair, 2002, p. 125)

In multi-congregation ministries communication methods will have been learned in individual communities and a new skill is needed to enable effective communication between congregations. This need for essential clear and attributable communication is emphasized throughout this book. Where communication is poor, misunderstanding, rumour and skewed interpretation become the unfortunate consequence. At worst the whole group of congregations may feel like independent units, either in 'drift' or in competition for the attention of the main minister of oversight.

The intuitive face of oversight

One unfortunate aspect of leadership can be the tendency to 'shoot from the hip', and to even take a pride in it. Repentance at leisure is not always an option, particularly for the leader who is constantly exposed to public scrutiny. Good intuitive decisions are the result of intensive training, a developed and reflective spirituality and a high degree of self-awareness. They arise from scrupulous preparation and from deeply held and refined values. Immediate decisions, often by necessity made in a split-second, are best made when subconscious elements inform what might seem no more than intuitive hunches.

Intuitive face
Enable boundaries to be crossed
See beyond the evidence
Learn to manage complexity
Critique through reflective practice
Adapt as evidence and experience build

Figure 16 The intuitive face of oversight

Enable boundaries to be crossed

The rather strange privilege of liminality has been used to describe one role of the reflective leader. The work of the priest or minister was described to me in this way:

> I feel that as *Bridge Builder* priesthood is about managing boundaries so from the Old Testament the priest is the boundary person. So on the Cross Jesus as the Great High Priest establishes the boundary between heaven and earth and that the Priesthood of All Believers is that people in whatever ministry they have got manage boundaries in their pastoral relationships and so on. The ordained priest manages boundaries at baptisms and funerals, marriages, giving absolution and so on and I think that beyond that there should be someone who manages the boundary as well in a very public way between Church and Society because of the profile he has. The priest hopefully manages the boundaries in one parish or one chaplaincy or whatever. (Grundy, 2014, p. 189)

An archdeacon identified some particular aspects of being a woman in her ecclesiastical post:

> A word I would use is liminality. There are things about being a woman which make my application to the work different. There is a serious question about whether you are thought to be doing

it properly if, also as a woman, you do it differently. There is no doubt that women coming into senior posts bring a new breadth of experience which is different from that brought by men. So by liminality I mean that I may well cross thresholds in a different way. (Grundy, 2014, p. 189)

What emerges with engaging and remarkable clarity in these two examples is that the reflective leader, engaged in public life in community, region or nation can enable individuals and public opinion feeling 'stuck' or wanting to change to move to another place. This privilege and responsibility link directly with the times when a leader uses the experience of oversight, and the energy it generates, to see new things and to encourage people to move in new directions.

See beyond the evidence

This goes to the heart of the theological exploration of oversight, and affirms the ability to see the application of an idea or a product beyond the initial understanding or what 'focus groups' might have suggested. It is the touch of inspiration which can be acquired by the reflective leader.

The best-known contemporary example of this kind of leadership is the late Steve Jobs. As the founder of Apple with Steve Wozniak he took the use of personal computers to a new place. Seeing that these devices had wider potential application than in a small part of business he created a market among people who did not yet know they needed them. The application of already known technology was moved into a worldwide market with the development of the iPad, iPhone and iPod. Remarkable in itself, this leadership ability was not restricted to the 'broad brush' approach to the running of companies favoured by a particular type of leader.

Steve Jobs was famous for the fanatical attention to detail he insisted on in the creation and promotion of his products. Since his early death in 2011 at the age of 56 there has been an increased interest in his personality and leadership qualities, which present an example of a necessary face of oversight in the work of the leader who takes a product, organization or group of people on to a new place. In intuitive and inspired ways he appeared to be able to predict the needs of customers and consumers and to know how to educate and entice them towards a future which he could predict long before they knew of it themselves.

Learn to manage complexity

The reflective and intuitive leader is able to see more than the 'sum of the parts' of what is described or observed. This takes a particular skill, whether gift or developed ability. What to one person can seem a confusing picture of complex and often contradictory situations and expectations can appear to another to present a challenging opportunity to create a new cohesiveness and interpretation. This has been summarized well by Tim Harle, the vice-chair of the church leadership organization MODEM. He says that there is a time when the leader can be 'comfortably out of control', when they can be looking for 'non-linear' solutions to emerge (Harle, 2011, p. 8).

Robin Greenwood has taken this complexity theory idea and related it to the Holy Trinity. He has focused on the rather difficult word 'perichoretic' to describe the fluctuating movement of relationships as instanced by the Trinity to illustrate how movement is achieved without overall chaos ensuing or of one group or person becoming dominant over another (Greenwood, 1994, p. 152).

The task of oversight at any level of responsibility is to ensure that competing demands do not cause an organization to descend into chaos, or stagnation, but energize it towards new life. Harle offers encouragement in the frustrating tasks of leadership; he regards 'change management' as one of the great oxymorons of the language of management (2011, p. 7). He maintains that the unexpected often brings growth, and occasionally a new and unexpected solution will emerge out of chaos or complexity. It is a skill of the leader to recognize this process and encourage and affirm a development, sometimes by providing resources at a key time. This is the type of 'leadership moment' spoken of by Blakely and Howard: when the time (*kairos*) is right the leader must not either fail to notice it or choose the wrong response (2010, p. 5).

Roxburgh and Romanuk make a helpful observation in *The Missional Leader* which affirms the organic nature of oversight. In their view, in order to encourage congregations to engage in mission an appropriate culture or atmosphere has to be created: 'missional leadership is about creating an environment within which the people of God in a particular location may thrive' (2010, p. 72). The people of God in this instance may be more than those who are at present members of a congregation.

Critique through reflective practice

Reflective practice is a discipline in itself which was made widely available as a concept by Donald Schön in *The Reflective Practitioner: How Professionals Think in Action* (1983). Building on work done by Lewin, James and Jung, and important for this face of oversight, he made the necessary connections between theory and practice, expressing his ideas through the use of diagrammatic modelling.

Creating learning environments requires a particular skill. In theological and ecclesiological language 'reflective practice' has come to be identified with the learning or 'pastoral cycle'. In everyday language this might be called 'learning from our mistakes'. More precisely it originates in a methodology developed by the Roman Catholic Church as part of its social teaching, providing a method of relating teaching, particularly in papal encyclicals, to everyday life.

Learning from our mistakes is too simplistic a description, though when things do go wrong we are forced to examine situations in more depth than when things go right. The pastoral cycle has as its great strength the fact that it engages with experience, and with the biblical and ecclesiastical tradition which nurture and inform us. It requires the development of the skill of reflective practice – and it gives us another chance to 'do it better', or at least differently, the next time!

The pastoral cycle (see Figure 17) has been developed in many different ways, most recently through work by Thompson and Thompson (2012) and by Tim Ling and Lesley Bentley (2012). They see in this diagrammatic model an enduring means of understanding our situations, working differently with others and drawing on different disciplines to enhance our work. This method of working provides a tool for reflection on activity so that more effective work and leadership can emerge. It draws into the experience of oversight the need to change and adapt; also, on occasions, to accept that a wrong decision has been made and that an acknowledgement of this is needed.

Figure 17 The pastoral cycle

Adapt as evidence and experience build

One core task of a leader is to 'create a path to another place', or perhaps 'build a bridge for others to cross', as described in the definition from Archbishop John Sentamu. It involves both skill and intuition, and to this definition can be added the comment by

Bishop Peter Price about needing to know where the path might lead. The leader with responsibility for several groups of people – congregations, diocese, district or region – can gain a much wider overall picture of what may be happening than those committed to working locally. This greater perspective, and with it the privilege of meeting many people from other walks of life and different professions and disciplines, will also give opportunities to revise opinions and give new leads.

Once again, the ability to reflect on one's situation and then know what to communicate and when is essential. It requires significant self-discipline and control. The temptation to rush in, intervene, make hasty decisions only to regret them later is present in the work of every leader.

The personal development face of oversight

Personal development is not introspection; it is the willingness to change and be changed by challenging experiences. Many resources are available to assist with this, both from external training agencies and from the constant search for frameworks and concepts which will make sense of situations for the leader who faces on a daily basis new and sometimes incomprehensible challenges. Integrated and assisted in their understanding, these experiences become the means by which personal development is achieved.

Personal development face
Develop self-understanding
Use external agencies
Use peer-groups and networks
Learn to know yourself
Depend on streams of spirituality

Figure 18 The personal development face of oversight

Develop self-understanding

It is in the area of self-understanding and spiritual awareness that leaders look for accessible tools to enable them to understand themselves and those they work alongside. It would be an unusual church leader who had not participated in one form of self-understanding or another, most often the Myers-Briggs personality type indicator. This accessible analysis, available through trained personnel, assesses the personality traits of introversion and extroversion. Self-understanding is not only a personal requirement. It is necessary across and between congregations in a wider grouping. This methodology is widely used for people who work in teams, and aims to understand the approaches of different personalities which are brought to the work.

Use external agencies

Many of those exercising ministries of oversight refer to the training or consultancy agencies which have influenced or shaped their analytical skills as they progressed through their careers or ministries. Since multi-congregation ministry is only just becoming recognized as a norm, it is hardly surprising that there are few denominational programmes for training, although such training is offered in some dioceses and by certain church societies and church-related agencies. Dadswell observes perceptively that it is easy for church leaders to dismiss outside consultants just because they think that the Church is an organization unlike any other. He reflects with some accuracy on a range of assumptions about the way in which churches traditionally operate which deserve challenge from good-quality secular theory. He concludes:

> Balance needs to be sought in knowing enough to be able to use the skills and insights ethically without having to be a world expert. The major benefit of calling on a range of disciplines is how they help to analyse a situation by looking at qualitatively different dynamics in explaining what is going on. The skill is not just in being able to do the analysis but also to work with the

complex, interacting impacts that the different analyses bring, assessing their relevance and significance. (Dadswell, 2011, p. 9)

Use peer-groups and networks

Much of what is emerging in this new ecclesiological situation comes from self-help networks, and from the exchange of best practice when ministers meet, perhaps for a completely unconnected reason. There are fewer than might be expected cross-responsibility groups and even fewer ecumenical support groups for leaders. It is here that the regional ecumenical agencies can have value. The importance of building up relationships is that when a crisis occurs there are colleagues available, people who can be trusted and can respond in an effective way.

There is undoubtedly a culture of self-help and peer support within many denominations. This has much to commend it and reflects well the entrepreneurial nature of many able leaders. What appears to be lacking is any centralized connection between individual activity, training agencies and diocesan or national training programmes. That lack of cohesiveness demonstrates an absence of the necessary theological and ecclesiological understandings of oversight. The establishment of these faces which encourage reflective practice and integrated development are an evidence-based foundation for integrated learning and professional development.

Learn to know yourself

This face of leadership reveals what resources are required to sustain the leader under pressure. Those who undertake oversight tasks need to have exceptional spiritual resources. In the words of St Bernard of Clairvaux, the Benedictine theologian and spiritual guide, 'Everyone has to drink from their own well'. This phrase was taken up by the liberation theologian Gustavo Gutierrez in his story of the spiritual journey working with the people of Lima in Peru. He contrasts the busy community experience of working alongside people to the necessary solitude or 'space' which an individual requires to keep their self-respect and for renewal.

The same can be said of any church leader, where public ministry requires them to take particular steps to resource themselves using a chosen spiritual tradition. For that resourcing to be 'earthed' and invigorated by the everyday concerns of their people, they need to relate and draw their authority from the community which gives them their office. Their own personal disciplines and resulting self-awareness will tell them that at the same time they need personal space and organized resources with which to renew themselves.

Savage and Boyd-Macmillan chose to explore wholeness and holiness and draw on the well of the humility of God in writing about how to shape the 'human face of the church':

> We underestimate the captivating *aliveness*, the delightful humour that is the humility of God. Divine humility is glimpsed through messy social processes: Jesus interacting with those around him. His unappetizing team of disciples tries out the new social rules; (love one another, confront, forgive, serve, *oops* try again). They emerge after his costly resurrection as empowered, courageous, but still leaky vessels. (Savage and Boyd-Macmillan, 2007, p. 225)

In the face of enormous challenges, personal development can easily be determined by the pressures of the work rather than by the ability to experience, interact and reflect on the challenges and opportunities the self-aware leader is presented with.

Depend on streams of spirituality

The spirituality of the Benedictine tradition has captured the imagination and met the needs of many leaders; in recent times it has been used in leadership training programmes. Pressurized businesspeople and church leaders looking to find space outside the public arena to make sense of their lives have found that the Benedictine balanced life of prayer and work addresses their needs. Speaking about Benedictine spirituality in a lecture at Trinity Church, Wall Street in New York in April 2003, Archbishop Rowan Williams pointed out that the chapters in the Rule on the abbot's ministry emphasize that the place and work of the person in authority is not to mediate between fixed groupings of people or opinions but to 'attend to the needs and strengths of each in such a way as to lead them forward harmoniously'. That is precisely the kind of attitude needed to exercise responsible oversight. It does not necessarily come naturally, but emerges from the rhythms of a life shaped by the kind of prayerful discipline which helps to understand what work in community is for and the purposes it can be designed to achieve.

A growing number of both lay and ordained people have been influenced by the spirituality and teaching, or 'principles', of St Francis. Archbishop Desmond Tutu is one of many senior people who, along with thousands of others, are members of the Third Order of the Society of St Francis. For those Christians in secular leadership the Christian Association of Business Executives (CABE) has taken the Principles of St Francis and turned them into a month of daily exercises designed for those who want practical application of Christian teaching as understood and interpreted by St Francis in their everyday lives.

It is important that any church leader should have some places which act as a spiritual frame of reference for them. These can appropriately be described as 'the wells from which we drink'. Benedictine or Franciscan spiritualities are two of many. All arise from reading the scriptural texts as a basic discipline. The denominational tradition, whether Anglican, Methodist, Baptist, Lutheran or Roman Catholic, needs to inform the spirituality of church leaders perhaps more than others since they are called to represent this tradition to their people.

Much spirituality transcends denominational boundaries, with its vitality and ability to speak to a common religious need. In this way people have been influenced by Celtic spirituality and the outworking of faith from the Iona Community. In terms of peace and reconciliation, the Corrymeela Community in Northern Ireland has been a source of spirituality. Some Christian leaders also now look to other faith traditions to feed and inform their spiritual journeys.

Church leaders sometimes face difficulties which can be traced to their choice or experience of spiritual tradition, if it is different from the main one which forms their denominational base and in which they are leaders. The purpose of a well-nurtured spirituality in a church leader has another dimension from solely that of a personal discipline. It is the essential element in ensuring that self-awareness is part of the leader's kitbag of essential tools. Separation from the colleagueship of others is the burden of the leader. The longer a person is in post the more they can run the risk of not being able to take advice and listen to the critical friends around them.

The default position face of oversight

It may seem too easy and simplistic to use a term from the language of computers to describe the principal fault of the leader under pressure. It describes the personality trait well. In all this development of oversight I have tried to join together secular language and concepts with those from theology and from the personal experience of many already engaged in ministry. In good times it is easy to be, or to appear to be, consultative. The formation in an internalized working method comes to the surface when a leader is under pressure. What can both undermine authoritative leadership and breed distrust is when a leader changes a professed style of operating because they come under pressure. This change may be necessary, but it requires patient explanation and a great amount of self-knowledge.

Default position face
Learn to lead with consistency under pressure
Understand the difference between consultation and manipulation
Learn to lead with integrity
Balance self-importance with humility
Keep the dots joined up

Figure 19 The default position face of oversight

Learn to lead with consistency under pressure

A good example of self-awareness and the way in which a leader responds to pressure was given by a Methodist District chair when describing other activities which contributed to his leadership skill:

> A lot of my leadership thinking comes from what I do in my spare time – I skipper sail training yachts. This is always with a team of other people. I thought it would be the other way round but at the beginning of a voyage I tend to be very participative but when things get stormy I say do it and ask the questions afterwards. I might go into the authoritarian mode when necessary and I do see that in me in parts of church life. (Grundy, 2014, p. 185)

A reversion to individualism or to a method of working from a different context is adopted in an uncritical way with an apparent absence of duplicity. This type of contradiction in leadership style is the primary reason for the evaporation of loyalty from colleagues. To operate in a collegial leadership style in good times and an authoritarian one in bad times demonstrates a lack of awareness of different default positions and the need for external and objective critique and evaluation.

Understand the difference between consultation and manipulation

Leaders who consult and adapt their vision are exercising sophisticated oversight and often a deep spiritual awareness. They know that consultation takes longer than persuasive decision-making; they are aware of the temptations of manipulation. However, the biggest perceived gap between the leader and those who are led is in the understanding of leadership styles and methods which are being used. While the leader may think that they are acting in everyone's best interests and the methods they use are legitimate, there may well be another perception unknown to the less self-aware. Experienced leaders are skilful in enabling change: they may be equally experienced and skilful in 'getting what they want' to happen. Leading with integrity requires an awareness of the default face of oversight where the possibility of manipulation for ease of decision-making is a real temptation.

Archbishop Rowan Williams states this with the voice of experience as someone who has had the welfare of the Church at the centre of his understanding of oversight.

> You must listen to what is actually going on so that when things change or move, it is the Body, not a group that is coerced or manipulated into following an agenda. So, if it is about following the direction of the Son of God, exercised in listening for what I've called the heartbeat of the Body of Christ, it is fairly risky because it's bound to have a rather long vision. (Foundation for Church Leadership, 2005, p. 5)

The perceived difficulty with leadership demonstrated by Williams is that too much listening and openness without decisive critical awareness can lead to vacillation, or to the support of a particular group in order to defend their vulnerability. Listening to the 'heartbeat of the Body of Christ' is a primary task for every Christian leader.

Learn to lead with integrity

Richard Higginson, director of the Ridley Hall Foundation for the Study of Faith in Business, has studied integrity as part of his analysis of the nature and quality of leadership (Higginson, 1996, pp. 54–8). He points out that integrity is a word which appears in a wide range of mission statements produced by commercial companies; the examples he gives are Cadbury-Schweppes, National Westminster Bank, the Ford motor company, British Petroleum, Shell, Hewlett-Packard, United Biscuits and British Aerospace. This must mean that the concept has some contemporary significance in the world of corporate ethics and has to have a particular relevance as a characteristic of ecclesiastical leadership. He also points out that throughout the Bible and particularly in Job and the Psalms it is used to describe 'righteousness' and 'uprightness' (Job 2.3; 2.9; 27.5; 31.6; Ps. 7.8; 25.21; 26.1). Higginson points out that not surprisingly integrity is a persistent and attractive 'virtue' in Proverbs: 'The integrity of the upright guides them, but the crookedness of the treacherous destroys them' (11.3); 'Better is a poor man who walks in his integrity than a man who is perverse in speech and is a fool' (19.1).

Higginson concludes that such frequent use of the word 'integrity' implies certain expectations of both the senior leader and the public or socially responsible company or church. These characteristics include fair dealing, vigilance over standards and about safety, and honesty in dealing with others. Each of these combines to build up trust and to give credibility to a person's actions and to the organization for which they are responsible.

It might be expected, or even assumed, that faith leaders have integrity. That is not always the case, and respect has to be won – often over and over again with every difficult decision which has to be made. No one coming into office can assume that the inherited qualities of their predecessors will automatically be conferred on them. Credibility and trust have to be earned, requiring experience fed by spirituality and by intellect. That is what the continuing process of formation and re-formation requires of each one of us and what I am attempting to set out in the many different aspects of oversight described here.

Balance self-importance with humility

Leaders often lament the sense of isolation which goes with the job and its responsibilities. To some extent this is a legitimate complaint, but creating distance which leads to isolation can be a deliberate role construction. This can be compounded by collusion between the leaders who want to feel that they are 'different' and their followers or staff who want to keep responsibility and the accountability which goes with leadership at arm's length. Particularly in church appointments hubris – the tendency towards exaggerated self-importance – can come with many years of service and long and unchallengeable senior appointments.

Dr David Owen, the former senior British politician and medical practitioner, has made an international study of the effects of long periods in power on political leaders (Owen, 2007). While he does not extend this to senior church leaders, many of the characteristics he describes can be recognized. One particular feature of senior leadership in the churches is that many are in the same post for more than seven years, and sometimes more than ten. This contrasts with senior managers in industry and commerce whose tenure is likely to be less than five years. Head teachers now have a similar time frame, as the pressures they encounter mean that many will be in post for less than seven years. Because church leaders are in post for longer than most of their senior colleagues, they can be more susceptible to certain identifiable characteristics or temptations arising from the isolation of their situation. It is possible to associate the succumbing to these types of 'temptations' to a lack of a structure for personal discipline and spiritual self-awareness. The leader, and especially the faith leader, needs to be well aware of the lifestyle factors contributing to hubris which can affect and change them. They need to take deliberate steps to prevent the onset or deepening of this behaviour.

It is very interesting to note that the medically trained Owen does not 'diagnose' the hubris syndrome as an inherent personality disorder, but as an obsessive behaviour characteristic caused by long stays in positions of leadership and thus in power with little external constraint on their actions. People surrounded by deference, at the top of a hierarchy, are inevitably prone to this syndrome, and can easily succumb to the temptations of power. On the other hand, if they rely on a well-constructed system of external reference and spiritual direction this can prevent them from the worst side of themselves – and perhaps of almost all of us.

The theologian Paul Tillich dwells in some detail on hubris in the second volume of *Systematic Theology*. He regards hubris as the ultimate estrangement of a person from God. This is in contrast to the understanding of all semblances of greatness as a small part of the privilege of being made in the image of God. The person with significant hubris sees themselves as the centre of their world and their own self-aggrandizement as the purpose of their work and the object of their elevated position:

> *Hubris* has been called the 'spiritual sin', and all other forms of sin have been derived from it, even the sensual ones. *Hubris* is not one form of sin beside others. It is sin in its total form, namely, the other side of unbelief or man's turning away from the divine centre to which he belongs. It is turning toward one's self as the centre of one's self and one's world. (Tillich, 1964, pp. 56–9)

Tillich's theological analysis combines elements of Greek tragedy where heroes try to emulate the gods, with biblical examples. The failure to resist temptation makes people fallible human beings, 'the mortals' who condemn themselves because they succumb to the temptation to make themselves like the gods, 'the immortals'. True Greek heroes are those who do not succumb to the sin of hubris but resist it and thus show their greatness. It is this that makes them stand out from the ordinary and the all too fallible.

Tillich moves on to the first and greatest biblical example at the very beginning of Genesis, where Adam and Eve are tempted through the serpent's promise that if they eat of the tree of knowledge they will become equal to God. He sees also one of the roles of the prophets as challenging kings and others in power over the misuse and abuse of power – caused by wanting to become like God rather than demonstrating humility and remembering their fallibility and the fragility of their position.

Keep the dots joined up

Writing after he had retired, Michael Adie described well the pressures and busyness of his work as a diocesan bishop, and lamented the lack of time to see patterns and links in the various aspects of his role. It was only in retirement that he was able to observe the need for 'cohesiveness' in reflection on ministry and the need to find time and an apparatus to enable connections to be made and understood (Adie, 1997). When time can be given to developing and understanding the significance of coherence, the value of 'joining up the dots' can be identified.

A reference to the necessary consultancy skills for work with multi-congregation ministries from David Dadswell emphasizes this point. Without a coherent understanding of the nature of resources and how best they might be deployed, a 'smorgasbord' method of working is likely to be the result. Those who work with groups need to be seen to be listening and learning just as much as those who use consultants to help understand their working situations.

The significance of developed faces of oversight

Once the four dynamic faces of oversight have been identified, resourced and developed then exciting new possibilities begin to emerge. They take this study on from evidence-based findings which are in themselves new and add to our knowledge of church and *episkope* in particular ways. The necessary qualities in potential ordinands, clergy and lay leaders can be identified. They have an essential significance in providing criteria for the selection of future leaders when put alongside the theological and ecclesiological understandings of *episkope* outlined in this study.

Possibly of the greatest importance in the long term is the way in which this development of the faces of oversight can be used to develop and sustain those called to work in places where the issues they face are both difficult and complex. Described in the essential features of these faces are the pitfalls and traps which exist for everyone called to be a leader or to exercise a ministry of oversight. The sense of isolation, the temptation to self-aggrandizement, the gradual reliance on solutions which have worked in previous posts, the reluctance to appoint creative and challenging staff, and much more, can be ameliorated when these generic characteristics are considered by those who support and advise church leaders.

For those whose responsibility it is to train and support leaders and to provide in-service training this concept of faces removes the temptation to 'pick and choose' courses and programmes.

The time of smorgasbord selectivity within training is over. In this developed grid there is a systematic programme for the training and support of leaders.

In a further development of my oversight grid, the four faces can form a reference point for review and accountability. So often clergy and senior leaders complain that they are not aware of the criteria by which they are being evaluated. New schemes address practicalities and the efficient carrying out of tasks. These faces, with their theological underpinning, now provide a theoretical basis for the understanding of senior leadership as a part of the general oversight which needs to be observed and understood in an episcopal church.

The biggest danger to any church, as in many other institutions, is a culture of individualism. In no way is it suggested that talented individuals are not needed or are expected not to bring their personality to their leadership of company, school or church. This chapter has attempted to provide structured ways in which the gifts within a talented personality can be nurtured, affirmed, encouraged and evaluated. Most significantly it presents a way in which leadership gifts can be maintained and shared to support and enable others while not being corrupted by the responsibilities and trappings of power.

6

A New Calling

It is now possible to enter this final phase of the in-depth examination of multi-congregation ministries with no more family secrets to be kept and with the vision of Alan Ecclestone continuing to inspire. His passionate desire was to see the congregation as 'a body of people drawn and held together in a spirit that prompts the members to care for, respect and love each other. It is the embodiment in any place of the I-in-You, You-in-Me relationship which Christ prayed for' (Ecclestone, 1997, p. 76). He was an energized dreamer with the great ability to set out the possibilities for how the Body of Christ might renew itself.

> Scattered among the people in our fragmented churches today are those who hunger for something other than that they see, who are in pain because the church they belong to seems hopelessly stuck fast in a way of life that by no stretch of imagination can be described in terms of leaven, or salt or light. (p. 77)

Such renewal has to be grounded in local ownership of a Church with much wider frames of reference. We hear the words of Roland Allen echoing through the decades: 'that object could only be attained if the first Christians who were converted by our labours understood clearly that they could by themselves, without any further assistance from us, not only convert their neighbours, but establish churches' (Allen, 1927, p. 64). It is to the successors of such people that this book has set out to speak.

This has not been an exercise in ecclesiastical archaeology. We began by looking at the origins of church order in the Christian faith because the right place to launch in was by exploring again

what was the original calling or founder's aim. The need to redis-
cover the original calling or 'charism' of a church or religious
order stems from a decree of the Second Vatican Council, in
the document *Renovationis Causam*, and was first suggested as
a foundation for wider ecclesiastical renewal, and as a basis for
consultancy work, by Peter Rudge. It has been possible to build a
case which demonstrates that something new is demanded of the
way in which local church congregations are understood.

While acknowledging the importance of Keith Elford's 'managing the present', which included the all-important 'know the
past', what needs to be worked at is his 'nurture identity' with
its consequent 'create the future'. Each is related to the other,
interacting and giving energy. These concepts and ideas accompany congregation members, local ministers of oversight and
denominational leaders on a journey, giving them an accessible
framework for progress and evaluation. It is this search for the
developing identity of multi-congregation ministries in a new
setting which has justified drawing on history and theology as well
as on ministerial practice. The need to establish a means of both
understanding and creating the future requires knowledge of the
theories which underpin best practice in various types of leadership and also the means to reflect using theological resources on
the kind of future which is emerging.

A relational theology of oversight

Emphasis has been placed on the relational nature of oversight in
multi-congregation situations and on particular ways of imple-
menting and supporting change. We may now be able to discover,
or rediscover, a unifying idea which will generate a strong sense of
community to counter the outflow of energy which is all too easily
diverted into deepening divisions. The identification of the different ways in which oversight can be understood in the historical
narrative provides an opportunity for a broader understanding
and further development.

A range of key words and concepts have been woven together to establish a sufficiently robust foundation on which to base a theological understanding and a practical application for local oversight in multi-congregation ministries. This is based on an assumption that one way of discerning the needs and hopes of congregations today can be by looking at the choices and concepts used by the first Christians in their adoption of a multi-layered word. *Episkope* or oversight was an appropriate description for the practical work and role imagined for leaders of groupings of congregations in the emerging Christian Church. It also expressed a profound theological understanding of the God of the Hebrew Scriptures who had brought about such a significant change in relationship to all of human society. Necessary importance has been given to the exploration of why and how this structure in Christian churches, which rapidly became hierarchical with its senior leaders exercising forms of monarchical episcopacy, endured through the centuries.

From this discussion it has been possible to make an essential transition to demonstrate that *episkope*, translated as oversight, could bear the weight of further development in a local situation where many congregations are joined together. This concept of oversight possesses the potential to form the theological and practical gateway which can reveal the relational and reciprocal nature of a church whose members and leaders have a rediscovered understanding of their obligation and responsibility to 'watch over one another in community'. Such a transition is possible but the 'memory' of what is needed has been forgotten or diminished and needs clarification and theological restatement as the nature of community comes to be understood in new ways. Local congregations and their clergy are to be encouraged to move on from individual local identity to new understandings of shared belonging and reciprocal caring. New structures to support this have been outlined in some detail. These lead to how an understanding of oversight can have practical and theological underpinning experienced as 'watching over one another in community'.

Oversight and Christian mission

The nature and mission of Christian churches derive from God and can only be worked out through the calling of the Church. Whether ministerial authority in episcopal churches has always to be traced by apostolic succession and validated before the exercise of an apostolic ministry can begin remains a subject for debate. At the personal level it is the way in which a leader relates to those in their charge which is of the greatest significance. The most appropriate way to describe this is through 'visitation', a concept which has its origin in *episkope* describing the actions and activity of God. The Old Testament uses of *episkope* are linked to the experiences of visitation because all contact with God was understood as in some sense relational and expresses feelings that people are cared for, protected, led and disciplined.

Arising from a perceived view of Christian mission found in the writings of sociologists who have concerned themselves with the work of Christian churches, a further avenue for future examination has emerged which is of considerable significance, particularly illustrated by the comments of Maddy Thung and others associated with post-colonial assertions about the future shape and tasks of the churches. Here the assumption was that Christian mission was not about 'proselytizing' but about equipping Christian individuals to transform their places of work and influence by personal commitment and example. This was also an assumption of Wickham and his followers in the work of industrial mission.

With church growth as a major item on the agenda for historic denominations, there is a concern about a change of influence from engagement with the world towards building up the nature and size of congregations. The new challenge is how these two important aspects of the Christian faith can be balanced. To relieve this very real tension the concept of liminality has been introduced. While acknowledging that this is an unusual and technical term it does have significance. The responsibility of oversight, not least in multi-congregation situations, is to accompany groups of people and congregations on to a new place. This gives a new dimension to the concept of mission. It is no longer solely a responsibility to 'make disciples' but now aims to bring individuals and groups to new understandings of how life in community can be experienced. Adoption of the fundamental interpretation of *episkope* as 'watching over one another in community' makes this possible.

Multi-congregation groupings can be reluctant to accept the new and unfamiliar, and there will be differing and contradictory views about how change should take place. They may or may not have a trusting relationship with those in wider denominational positions of power. For ministers of oversight, adopting the role of accompanier and at times conceptual leader is a great privilege and responsibility. It is fundamental to be aware that there are aspects of the nature of God, as creator, shepherd, servant and much more, which can be embraced in the exploration of liminal leadership and oversight.

Ecumenism and the renewal of oversight

In the search for understandings and applications of oversight, we have seen that one of the most fundamental discoveries was the extent to which *episkope* has featured in ecumenical dialogue and agreement. This is as important in the life of the local church as it is in national co-operation – and just as easy to ignore! In ecumenical documents and agreements *episkope* has been described as having core characteristics which arise from the community and the common life of the Church described as *koinonia*. The nature of its *apostolicity* stems from a continuity of the commission from the first apostles and its underlying *unity* through the universally accepted and recognized sacrament of baptism. Regarding the responsibilities within ministerial practice there is ecumenical agreement that *episkope* is exercised by its leaders *personally*, *collegially* and *communally*. Continuing exploration has included the need to clarify and develop the relationship within reciprocal oversight or *episkope* between church members and their leaders. The next phase will be the rediscovery of what transformed and former 'hierarchical' relationships will look like. This exploration will bring anxiety to some about the loss of role and status, while liberating others from feeling 'imprisoned' by expectations which are no longer appropriate.

Metaphor and mind pictures of oversight

We have looked at oversight images described in secular theory, biblical narrative and by current practitioners. Three overarching oversight concepts were devised from a long list of suggested images and metaphors. When categorized and grouped, these formed a template which can be placed over the activity of any large organization as a means of analysis or review. In the local church, with appointed leaders and teams, these 'mind pictures' have three differing but essential recognizable characteristics:

> ➢ They describe oversight in ways which enable individuals and communities to grow in an organic way.
> ➢ People under authority or groups committed to the development of an organization need to have the sense that they are going somewhere together.
> ➢ Oversight has to be authoritative and carry with it integrity which earns respect for the office as much as for the person.

Drawn together, these three 'generic' concepts led to the proposal of an 'oversight grid' made up of combined and grouped descriptions of the essential components for effective oversight. This was extended to form a dynamic construct of four 'faces' and developed to introduce resources for personal ministerial formation. These suggested creative and innovative solutions will be useful for sustaining those called to multi-congregation ministry. They consisted of *the public face, the intuitive face, the personal development face and the default face* of an understanding, which could assist in the formation, support and evaluation of those in oversight roles. This exploration was based on findings in theoretical, historical, biographical and practical research, and much material which has been researched or offered by others took on a new and vigorous life providing both formation and ongoing ministerial support. In this combination of ideas, experience and resources those called to leadership, and those who select and train leaders, may be helped to discover not only where their roles and responsibilities lie but also where to find the resources of consultancy which are needed to develop and sustain those called to ministries of participative oversight.

This theological and practical framework for the understanding of the structure or ecclesiology of churches suggests that the divisions and disputes within local and national churches could be diminished with a renewed commitment to reciprocal and relational oversight. The interpretation of oversight as 'watching over one another in community' may offer a way to redefine the fundamental ethos of life in our historic denominations, and fill the space between centralized, bureaucratic or hierarchical leadership and congregationalism or party and alternative church groupings.

Consequently, and for the same reasons, we can conclude that those with the task of conducting reviews and planning reconstruction of the historic denominations need to have a clear frame of reference within which to work. Appropriate pathways for formation and training are essential for the development and subsequent consolidation of the work of senior leaders so that they can hold on to a renewed understanding of the nature of oversight.

Theology before practice

The ways in which church structures are created and ministries formed need always to reflect renewed theological understandings of a foundational charism. There will be much anxiety, many experiments, some failures and many successes before consolidated change can be recognized, affirmed and legitimated. Such experiences are described visually and effectively in John Fisher's 'transition curve' (2005).

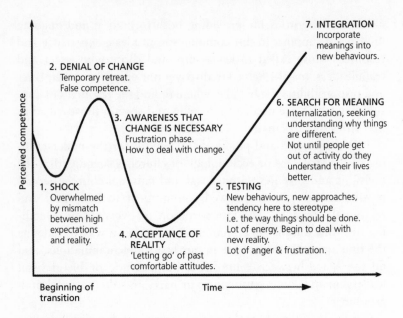

Figure 20 The transition curve

This diagram (see Figure 20) describes precisely the outworking of John Adair's concept of development in *The Becoming Church*: that churches are always 'becoming something different'. An understanding of the stages of the emotional processes of change provides analysis within a framework which is both practical and strategic. As transition continues to take place there is much to celebrate about this new situation in our churches. A few examples are described below.

Faith hubs

Faith hubs are what multi-congregation ministries have become in practice. They give support to local congregations and establish much needed local identity to communities undergoing change. More than anything else their virtue lies in that they are local. They take the name of their locality, and the specific choice of name and accompanying logo can create a new identity and express how people understand the changing nature of their own communities. A prophetic choice acknowledged by many can move the self-understanding of whole communities on to a new place. Such foundational work reflects directly the role of oversight from the earliest days. The original work of the local *episkopos* exercising oversight was to hold a centre ground, ensure fairness and integrity in community activity, oversee the fair distribution of resources to those in need, and prevent inward-looking activities in order that local Christian communities extended hospitality to all.

Community support networks

Churches and their congregations are often the main unifying component of a group of communities. In many places they share this role to some degree with schools and village halls. The establishment of community support networks gives a strengthened voice to local people. Often the local church, in this new grouping and wearing its ecumenical clothing, is the only trusted body which can voice and act on local concerns. In rural areas it will be the church building which offers hospitality to farming communities, for example for funerals which can be major events. Urban and civic churches will be asked to host commemorations, celebrations and opportunities for grieving in an increasingly significant way. In public ways and with appropriate local pastoral follow-up, community support networks can be created and developed. At times of crisis the extent to which the church with its local presence is expected to respond remains remarkable.

Barometers for local opinion

Local churches remain the one presence which covers the whole of a country. In local groupings feelings about community issues can be sensed with some accuracy and, where appropriate, voiced. Often, it is the local church which can speak out on a strongly felt issue or hold public discussion where the weight of opinion can be measured. With civic, regional and national connections accurate information can be used to inform and influence wider policy. The scale of rural and urban deprivation and hardship can be substantiated with real stories. Local trusts and community funds can be established with other partners to meet immediate community needs.

Workshops for liturgy

The development and exchange of good practice, not least in the appropriate and varied use of liturgies, makes local congregations networks for creativity. In a large grouping there is both space for the preservation and imaginative use of traditional liturgies and opportunity for experiment, which can reflect local need. Thoughtful and well-constructed liturgy demonstrates the outward work and concerns of a congregation. The often passionately held views of congregation members about their own work and their contribution to the community can be voiced best in the ways in which these concerns are translated into the spirituality of worship.

While core liturgies may retain a common structure there is much variation in how they are interpreted. New forms of less structured worship are developing across all denominations. In multi-congregation groupings wider resources become available; different congregations, each with their own age profile and approach to mission, may begin to specialize in particular ways, which will bring benefit to all. There is a major oversight role for the senior minister and leadership team in enabling balanced and appropriate development.

Shapers of community identity

Churches are the embodiment and repository of community identity and memory. The great advantage of being grouped in appropriate ways is that memory can be honoured, shared and celebrated. Continuity can be safeguarded, since communities can bring 'checks and balances' to one another. This is done very locally and by attendance or absence disapproval can be displayed in covert or very public ways. The grouping of ministers means that when one leaves there remains continuity rather than dramatic changes of personality and policy. Social and economic differences, local rivalries and aspirations can be levelled in the equality experienced when those who otherwise differ 'come to church together'.

Springboards for development

From this heritage of faith which is both ancient and modern we have deduced needs and responsibilities within oversight. These have been expanded by describing the expressed views of congregations or organizations. The purpose of vibrant Christian communities is to enable individuals to grow and develop, for all to experience a sense of direction and for boundaries to be known and on occasion crossed. This corporate activity enables just that possibility of growth and the movement on to new places.

Through this means of evaluation, culminating in affirmations of prophetic presence, a new approach has been established. It begins in an outline description of how congregations are related to one another and goes on to add the ways in which the minister, clergy or ministry team relate to each local congregation and to one another. It then uses the theological and organizational tools outlined in these chapters to arrive at an assessment of which features of oversight in community can be described as revealing something of the nature of God. It can also assess those elements of community life across congregations which enable growth, direction and outreach and which enrich our understanding of the ways in which our denomination is developing. From this the working relationship of lay groups and clergy can be assessed. This relates to the nature of leadership within multi-congregation ministerial situations. It informs, supports and evaluates the role and work of the senior leader responsible for local oversight. The criteria of individual, collegial and communal leadership come into play as objective means for effective evaluation.

Landscapes of transcendence

In a most affirming way, as this wide-ranging and critical appraisal of the problems and opportunities within multi-congregation ministries is concluded, I can say that when they work well they are real 'landscapes of transcendent culture'. By the very nature of partnership between groups of congregations in the context of their wider communities a patchwork of landscape, architecture, industry, commerce, leisure and local activity is brought together. Each has its own identity, sometimes shaped by generations, and always the object of hope and aspiration. By the contribution of integrated faithful communities another dimension can be added.

Three vocational questions

Three questions now remain which need to be explored concerning the nature of vocation in multi-congregation ministries. These are, first, what is the vocation of the local congregation and its partners in this new venture? Second, what is the new nature of a calling for ministers who are working and who will work in these new situations? Third, what will be the changed oversight responsibilities of our denominations as they come to terms with an understanding of church which is unlike any other before? In each it is essential not to rush into new solutions and to devise new policies and structures. Before all this comes the patient listening to the call from God; then we can begin to discern, often from the changes local congregations are experimenting with, what the shapes will be in this emerging church with its many families, communities and partners.

What is the new vocation for the local congregation?

In many ways a local congregation will look and feel much as it did before, or that will be the impression given on the surface. Regular services will take place in most congregations on every Sunday of the year. There may be a variety of worship through a month, and the style of worship for which that congregation is known will continue. In any case what is offered will be an attempt at the very best possible in the circumstances and with the resources available. There will be community events and ecumenical cooperation as before. Local organizations, cultural groups and schools will be welcome to use the building.

What will be different is the structure which supports this effective local presence. The main source of coordination for activities between 'partner' congregations will not be the full-time stipendiary minister but more likely the administrator for the group, whether paid or voluntary. What the minister with overall responsibility for oversight will be observing as collegial relationships become established is the appropriate and emerging balance between organic, directional and authoritative activity. Different, as we have already observed, is that clergy and lay ministers will have local pastoral responsibility but will probably rotate around congregations on Sundays. This will give variety and make the most of the skills ministers have. Different also will be that a named person, possibly ordained but equally likely a local layperson or pastoral group, will be responsible for immediate pastoral care which will continue to be offered to all in the local community. That person may well have the authority to decide which pastoral requests can best be met locally and which need to be referred to a member of the clergy and to the minister with overall oversight responsibility. All combine to give a broader and richer interpretation of how shepherding can be done is these rapidly adapting situations.

The vocation for all in the local congregation will have as its essence a developing understanding of how to move from dependence on clerical ministries towards not independence but interdependence. This fits completely with the understanding of local oversight which has been defined as 'watching over one another in community'. It is only the actual experience of doing this which proves its worth. Talking about what working in new ways 'might' be like only raises apprehension and fear. Once tried and developed not only does this seem a rich new way, in which there is much more to gain than to lose, but there comes the realization that cooperation in a range of ways can broker in additional resources of many kinds, both internally within the church community – family workers, children's workers, group evangelists, joint magazine editors, joint choirs, administration for funerals across the grouping, website managers – and externally, with conservation groups, voluntary organizations and many more with a balance which will fit particular local situations.

What is the new vocation for multi-congregation ministers?

What is new, and already a reality for many of those who are ordained, is that they will no longer be working as the only minister with a congregation. The generations-old culture of individualism which has pervaded clerical life is coming to an end. Some kind of staff group will be established, and the much-discussed theological concept of collegiality will be worked out within the local grouping. The calling to be a deacon or priest remains but is developed or transformed in this new context. It should be remembered that clergy have never worked 'alone', but have always had lay members of their congregations as colleagues – and still do!

There are significant consequences for a sense of personal vocation. Which of these new kinds of ministry is God calling a person towards? For vocations advisers and selectors in their panels there is the need to discern the type of ministry which would best match a candidate's skills and abilities – as well as their potential for development. The pastoral, sacramental and preaching ministries of clergy are set in this broader context. For those formed in the ways of individual-congregation ministry this may be a challenge, while for others it will be liberating. We have seen that people with specialist skills can feel affirmed and fulfilled in new ways, and those who felt 'trapped' by parochial duties in a relatively 'flat' organization will welcome the opportunity to work on a broader stage.

The difficult question of 'ambition' emerges more strongly when a new structural concept for oversight is introduced for local groupings of churches. Some candidates are already likely to have the skills and experience to manage and lead large groupings but because of a strong bias towards personal pastoral ministries may be reluctant to include this experience in a description of their call to ministry. Indeed, selectors might be suspicious if a candidate for ministry suggested this as a principal driver in their sense of vocation. However, vocations advisers and those who select and train ministers need to understand how different kinds of previous experience can give the potential for wider local leadership. It is possible for such ministers – and for every Christian – to recognize that their vocation can change or grow and develop as God and the Church call them to new ministries.

Some clergy will see a fulfilling vocation in offering 'team support', perhaps especially in being close to the ground in enabling and ministering to local Christians. Success and failure in the work of ministry become inappropriate concepts. Fulfilment comes in the discovery and explanation of different but complementary tasks and roles. These different roles which can all bring vocational satisfaction and fulfilment need to be understood by senior leaders with oversight. It is a new and salutary piece of learning that a vocation can be fulfilled in a range of team roles. A parallel development of vocation will be experienced by retired clergy as they bring a lifetime of experience to assist in the work and life of local congregations in new and challenging ways.

What is the new vocation for our denominations?

This is not the place to set out on a reform of dioceses and denominations. This examination has concentrated on changes in local congregations and from this it is suggested that most change will be organic and from the bottom up. Dioceses and denominations will adapt and legitimate change. Structures will be re-formed, there will be less bureaucracy, fewer meetings will be on weekdays and in the daytime, more decisions will be made by local groupings and there will be a much greater sense that oversight is shared. Most importantly, senior staff will see one of their chief responsibilities as the support of clergy placed in vulnerable and stressful situations as they attempt to pioneer new ways to minister in large groupings of congregations.

The image of shepherd has enduring significance both as a model and as a positive image for the work of oversight. There are, however, reservations about adopting this image as a personal model; some church leaders state that they only use the image of shepherd when speaking about Jesus, and not at any other time. The balance between shepherd and servant needs to be retained. Reflection on the self-understanding which Jesus had of his own ministry and of God's purposes within it brings us to the conclusion that 'while Christ is the King he is the Servant King'. John Rawsthorne, the former Roman Catholic Bishop of Hallam in South Yorkshire, expressed his unease with applying the model of shepherd to himself:

> It's funny isn't it I shy away and I should not because it is very scriptural. The problem with shepherd is sheep and I do not want our people to be sheep. I want them to be mature, responsible Christians and it is a difficult image. (Grundy, 2014, p. 195)

It remains probable that in our fallen world generally received positive images will continue to be manipulated to serve the needs of leaders who want themselves to be the focus of their work. The need for clear communication through shared language and concepts has yet to be fully understood by Church leaders as they reinterpret their responsibilities of shepherding. It is essential that they feel that they are reshaping a diocese or denomination which is working at theology and practice in a similar way to the local clergy, in order to give a greater sense of connectedness. Many in senior positions know that change is necessary but lack the necessary theological and reflective apparatus for confident change to be guided and affirmed. These new theological and structural understandings can be applied widely in national churches in the discernment of vocation and the subsequent identification of those yet to be appointed as senior ministers. They could offer a means of establishing criteria for those who encourage or discern vocation to a new and wider variety of ministries.

Bishops, archdeacons and regional ministers with their special-ist advisers will gradually come to discover that the need to be dynamic leaders who initiate and 'lead from the front' lessens, and they have a new local oversight group of colleagues with whom they can consult and share their responsibilities in a practical and theological way. The contribution of senior women leaders will at the very least influence the ways in which decisions are made and the nature and style of the interpretation and exercise of over-sight. All may learn the hard lesson that fewer initiatives will be initiated centrally or personally by individuals. Leaders may redis-cover the original 'charism' of their work, as devised by the first Christian communities which grouped themselves together. The task of oversight, then as now, is to ensure the equal distribu-tion of resources, the support of those in local congregations with their ministers, and the faithful communication of best practice across the wider Church. Being 'leaders in mission' meets a pres-ent need but may be no more than the application of a current interpretation of an imperative within oversight.

A prophetic presence

Having listened, analysed, reflected and proposed ways of under-standing and living in multi-congregation situations, robust markers for progress have emerged. Some are appropriate to most situations, while for others their greater or lesser significance will depend on local circumstance. Creative and dedicated people have given enormous amounts of time and energy to establishing new relationships within quite different structures. Cumulatively these are energizing and prophetic. Most have yet to be affirmed and internalized by their denominations. They are both the shape of things now and the springboard for things to come. In an energiz-ing and affirming way we can now describe some of these shapes. Others who are intimately involved in multi-congregation minis-tries, and who observe this work in their local communities, may well be able to add more.

Listening to the heartbeat of the Body of Christ

Whether the Church is an organization or an institution, it has been known from the days of St Paul as the Body of Christ on earth. This body has been much bruised and abused, broken again and again, but because it is the Church of the resurrection it has been consistently restored and re-formed. In multi-congregational ministries the metaphor of oversight has been enriched. These groupings bring together differing and complementary ministries to form one reshaped ministry. This contribution to this new way of functioning, through a renewed calling or vocation, has been the exploration of the fundamental nature of oversight. If nothing else, it has revealed the need for congregations and denominations, with their ministers, to commit themselves in new ways to 'watch over one another in community', and from this to add a new dimension to the life of the communities they serve.

Bibliography

Church of England Reports (in date order)

Central Advisory Council for Ministry, *Partners in Ministry: Being the Report of the Commission on the Deployment and Payment of the Clergy*, Chair W. Fenton Morley, Church Information Office, London, CA1640, 1967.

Advisory Council for the Church's Ministry, *A Strategy for the Church's Ministry*, Chair John Tiller, CHP, London, 1983.

Faith in the City: The Report of the Archbishop of Canterbury's Commission on Urban Priority Areas, CHP, London, 1985.

Church of England House of Bishops, *Faith in the Countryside*, A report for the Archbishops' Commission on Rural Areas, Churchman Publishing, Worthing, 1990.

Church of England House of Bishops, *Apostolicity and Succession*, GS Misc 432, House of Bishops Occasional Paper, General Synod of the Church of England, London, 1994.

Church of England House of Bishops, *Working as One Body*, The report of the Archbishops' Commission on the organization of the Church of England, Chair Michael Turnbull, CHP, London, 1995.

Church of England House of Bishops, *Bishops in Communion: Collegiality in the Service of the Koinonia of the Church*, SS Misc 580, House of Bishops Occasional Paper, CHP, London, 2000.

Archbishops' Council, *Challenges for the Quinquennium*, GS 1895, CHP, London, 2013; *Making New Disciples*, GS Misc 1054, CHP, London, 2012.

Archbishops' Council, *From Anecdote to Evidence: Findings from the Church Growth Research Programme 2011–2013* (www.churchgrowthresearch.org.uk).

Ecumenical reports (in date order)

Report of the Anglican–Methodist Unity Commission, SPCK and Epworth Press, London, 1968.

World Council of Churches, *Baptism, Eucharist and Ministry*, Faith and Order Paper No. 111, WCC, Geneva, 1982.

ARCIC (Anglican–Roman Catholic International Commission), *The Gift of Authority*, London, Rome, Section 36, 1988.

Council for Christian Unity, *The Porvoo Common Statement*, Council for Christian Unity of the Church of England, London, Occasional Paper No. 3, 1993.

Roman Catholic Bishops' Conference of England and Wales, *Catechism of the Catholic Church*, Geoffrey Chapman, London, 1994.

Roman Catholic Bishops' Conference of England and Wales, *The Sign We Give*, A report from the Working Party on Collaborative Ministry for the Catholic Bishops Conference of England and Wales, 1995.

The Nature of Oversight: Leadership, Management and Governance in the Methodist Church in Great Britain and *What is a District Chair?*, Minutes of Conference, Epworth Press, London, 2005.

Lund Statement, *Episcopal Ministry within the Apostolicity of the Church*, Lutheran World Federation, Stockholm, 2007.

Roman Catholic Church, *Anglicanorum Coetibus*, Congregation for the Doctrine of the Faith, Rome, 2009.

Theses and articles

Alberts, D. S. and Hayes, R. E., *Understanding Command and Control*, Command and Control Research Programme, U.S. Department of Defense, 2006.

Avis, P., 'Establishment and the Mission of a National Church', *Theology*, Jan/Feb 2000, SPCK, London.

Becker Sweeden, N., Book Review, Boston University School of Theology, Centre for Practical Theology, 2014, of N. Healy, *Church, World and Christian Life: Practical-Prophetic Ecclesiology*, CUP, Cambridge, 2000.

Bowes, P., *Future Church: Envisioning the Church of England in Southern Rydale in the Second Decade of the 21st Century*, Durham University, DMin Thesis, 2012.

Day, Jane, *What can Secular Feminism Contribute to the Development of Women Leaders in the Baptist Denomination?*, York St John University, MA Thesis, 2013.

Francis, L., Robbins, M. and Ryland, A., 'Do Introverts Appreciate the Same Things as Extraverts Within a Ministry Team? A study among leaders within the New Frontiers network of churches in the United Kingdom', *Social Scientific Study of Religion* (22), 2011, pp. 306–14.

Grundy, M., *Episkope as a Model for Leadership and Oversight in the Church of England Examined in the Dioceses of Yorkshire*, University of Leeds, PhD Thesis, 2014.

Jackson, M., 'Major Issues in Industrial Mission', *International Review of Mission*, WCC, Geneva, 54(214), Apr 1965, pp. 151–60.

Marshall, J., 'Images of Changing Practice through Reflective Action Research', *Journal of Organizational Change Management*, 24(2), 2011, pp. 244–56.

Mayer, J. and Salovey, P., 'The Intelligence of Emotional Intelligence', *Intelligence*, 17(4), 1993, pp. 433–42.

Rimmer, C., *Towards an Ecumenical Theology of Wilderness: Prospects for Ecumenism in the 21st Century*, WCC 60th Anniversary essay contest, WCC, Geneva, 2009.

Roomi, M. A. and Harrison, P., 'Entrepreneurial Leadership: What is it and how should it be taught?', *International Review of Entrepreneurship*, 9(3), Senate House Publishing, London, 2011.

Saarinen, M. F., *The Life Cycle of a Congregation*, Alban Institute, Action Information, May/June 1986; *The Life Cycle of a Congregation*, Alban Institute booklet AL88, Alban Publishing, Washington, 1996.

Stevenson, K., 'What the Fathers Might Say about Episcopacy Today', *Theology*, 114(2), Mar/Apr, 2011, SPCK, London.

Truscott, J., *The Leader as a Shepherd*, Research Papers A12 and A13 (www.john-truscott.co.uk).

General bibliography

Adair, J., *Action Centred Leadership*, Pan Macmillan, London, 1973.

Adair, J., *The Becoming Church*, SPCK, London, 1976.

Adair, J., *How to Find Your Vocation: A Guide to Discovering the Work You Love*, Canterbury Press, Norwich, 2000.

Adair, J., *Effective Strategic Leadership*, Pan Macmillan, London, 2002.

Adie, M., *Held Together: An Exploration of Coherence*, DLT, London, 1997.

Allen, R., *The Spontaneous Expansion of the Church*, World Dominion Press, New York, 1927, 1962.

Allen, R., *Missionary Methods: St Paul's or Ours?* World Dominion Press, New York, 1962.

Allen, R. and Paton, D., *Reform of the Ministry: A Study in the Work of Roland Allen*, Lutterworth, London, 1968, 2002.

Arbuckle, G., *Refounding the Church: Dissent for Leadership*, Geoffrey Chapman, London, 1993.

Avis, P., *Authority, Leadership and Conflict in the Church*, Mowbray, London, 1992.

Avis, P., *A Ministry Shaped by Mission*, T & T Clark, London, 2005.

Avis, P., *Beyond the Reformation? Authority, Primacy and Unity in the Conciliar Tradition*, T & T Clark, London, 2006.

Avis, P., *The Identity of Anglicanism: Essentials of Anglican Ecclesiology*, Bloomsbury, 2008, 2013.

Avis, P., *Reshaping Ecumenical Theology: The Church Made Whole?*, T & T Clark, London, 2010.

Barrett, Clive (ed.), *Unity in Process: Reflections on Ecumenism*, DLT, London, 2012.

Barry, F., *Period of My Life*, Hodder & Stoughton, London, 1970.

Bayes, P. and Sledge, T., *Mission-Shaped Parish: Traditional Church in a Changing Context*, CHP, London, 2006.

Bede, *A History of the English Church and People*, tr. L. Shirley-Price, Penguin Classics, London, 1955.

Beeson, T., *Rebels and Reformers: Christian Renewal in the Twentieth Century*, SCM, London, 1999.

Belbin, R., *Management Teams: Why They Succeed or Fail*, 3rd edn, Butterworth Heinemann, London, 2010.

Belbin, R., *Team Roles at Work*, 2nd edn, Butterworth Heinemann, Portsmouth, NH, 2010.

Berger, P., *The Social Reality of Religion*, Penguin, 1967.

Berger, P., *A Rumor of Angels*, Doubleday Anchor, Garden City New York, 1970.

Berger, P. and Luckmann, T., *The Social Construction of Reality*, Penguin, London, 1966, 1991.

Billington, W., *Growing a Caring Church: Practical Guidelines for Pastoral Care*, BRF, Abingdon, 2010.

Blakely, C. and Howard, S., *The Inner Life of a Christian Leader*, CPAS Leadership Series L2, Grove, Coventry, 2010.

Boulard, F., *An Introduction to Religious Sociology*, trans. M. J. Jackson, DLT, London, 1960.

Boyd-Macmillan, E. and Savage, S., *Transforming Conflict*, FCL, York, 2008.

Bramley, H., *Liber Regulae Pastoralis*, St Gregory, Pope, *c.* 590, J. Palmer, Oxford, 1874.

Brookes, S. and Grint, K., *The New Public Leadership Challenge*, Macmillan, Basingstoke and New York, 2010.

Bultmann, R., *Theology of the New Testament*, SCM, London, 1962.

Cameron, H., *Resourcing Mission: Practical Theology for Changing Churches*, SCM, London, 2010.

Carpenter, J., *Gore: A Study in Liberal Catholic Thought*, Faith Press, London, 1960.

Carr, W., *The Priestlike Task*, SPCK, London, 1985.

Casper, W., *Harvesting the Fruits: Basic Aspects of Christian Faith in Ecumenical Dialogue*, Continuum, London and New York, 2009.

Cavanagh, L., *By One Spirit: Reconciliation and Renewal in Anglican Life*, Peter Lang, Oxford, Bern and New York, 2009.

Cherry, S., *Barefoot Disciple: Walking the Way of Passionate Humility*, Continuum, London and New York, 2011.

Cherry, S., *Beyond Busyness*, Sacristy Press, Durham, 2012.

Cocksworth, C. and Brown, R., *Being a Priest Today: Exploring Priestly Identity*, Canterbury Press, Norwich, 2002.

Collins, J., *Are All Christians Ministers?* Liturgical Press, Collegeville, MN, 1992.

Collinson, D., Grint, K. and Jackson, B., *Leadership*, Sage, Los Angeles and London, 2011.

Covey, S. R., *The Seven Habits of Highly Effective People*, Fireside, Simon & Schuster, New York, 1989, 2000.

Croft, S., *Ministry in Three Dimensions*, DLT, London, 1999.

Croft, S., *Focus on Leadership*, FCL, York, 2005.

Croft, S., *Transforming Communities: Re-Imagining the Church for the 21st Century*, DLT, London, 2002.

Dadswell, D., *Consultancy Skills for Mission and Ministry*, SCM, London, 2011.

Dale, R., *A Manual of Congregational Principles*, John Murray, OUP, Oxford, 1884.

Davie, G., *Religion in Britain since 1945: Believing Without Belonging*, Blackwell, Oxford, 1994.

Davie, G., *Religion in Modern Europe: A Memory Mutates*, OUP, Oxford, 2000.

Davie, G., *Religion in Britain: A Persistent Paradox*, Wiley-Blackwell, Oxford, 2015.

Davies, M. and Dodds, G., *Leadership in the Church for a People of Hope*, T & T Clark/Continuum, London and New York, 2011.

Davis, H., *Pastoral Care*, Paulist Press, New York, 1950.

Donaldson, W., *Word and Spirit: The Vital Partnership in Christian Leadership*, BRF, London, 2011.

Downs, W., *The Parish as a Learning Community*, Paulist Press, New York and Toronto, 1979.

Drane, J., *The McDonaldization of the Church*, DLT, London, 2000.

Drane, J., *After McDonaldization: Mission, Ministry and Christian Discipleship in an Age of Uncertainty*, DLT, London, 2008.

Dulles, A., *Models of the Church*, Gill & Macmillan, London, 1974, 1987.

Ecclestone, A., *Staircase for Silence*, DLT, London, 1977.

Ecclestone, G. (ed.), *The Parish Church? Explorations in the Relationship of the Church and the World*, Mowbray, London, 1988.

Edgell Becker, P., *Congregations in Conflict: Cultural Models of Local Religious Life*, CUP, Cambridge, 1999.

Edmondson, C., *Leaders Learning to Listen*, DLT, London, 2010.

Edwards, D., *Leaders of the Church of England 1828–1944*, OUP, Oxford, 1971.

Elford, K., *Creating the Future of the Church: A Practical Guide to Addressing Whole Systems Change*, SPCK, London, 2013.

Evans, G. and Percy, M., *Managing the Church? Order and Organization in a Secular Age*, Sheffield Academic Press, Sheffield, 2000.

Finney, J., *Finding Faith Today*, British and Foreign Bible Society, London, 1992.

Fisher, J. M., 'A Time for Change', *Human Resource Development International*, 8(2), 2005, pp. 257–64.

Foundation for Church Leadership, *Focus on Leadership*, ed. M. Grundy, FCL, York, 2005.

Francis, L., *Faith and Psychology: Personality, Religion and the Individual*, DLT, London, 2005.

Francis, L. and Robbins, M., *Personality and the Practice of Ministry*, Pastoral Series P97, Grove, Cambridge, 2004.

Francis, L., Robbins, M., and Astley, G., *Fragmented Faith?* Paternoster Press, London, 2005.

Francis, L., Littler, K. and Martineau, J., *Rural Ministry: A Parish Workbook on Lay Ministry in the Country Church*, Acora Publishing, Warwick, 2000.

Fraser, I., *Reinventing Church: Insights from Small Christian Communities and Reflections on a Journey Among Them*, private publication, 2003.

Friedman, E., *Generation to Generation: Family Process in Church and Synagogue*, Guilford Press, New York and London, 1985.

Furlong, M., *The C of E: The State It's In*, SPCK, London, 2000.

Gibbs, E., *I Believe in Church Growth*, ed. M. Green, Barnes and Noble, New York, 1981.

Gibbs, E. and Bolger, R. K., *Emerging Churches: Creating Christian Communities in Postmodern Cultures*, Baker Academic, New York, 2005.

Gibson, T., *Church and Countryside: Insights from Rural Theology*, SCM, London, 2010.

Gill, R., *The Social Context of Theology*, Mowbray, Oxford, 1975.

Gill, R., *Theology and Social Structure*, Mowbray, Oxford, 1977.

Goleman, D., *Emotional Intelligence: Why It Can Matter More Than IQ*, Bantam Books, New York, 1995.

Gore, C., *The Church and the Ministry*, Green & Co., 1886, revised edition SPCK, London, 1936.

Gore, C., *Orders and Unity*, John Murray, London, 1909.

Greenwood, R., *Transforming Priesthood*, SPCK, London, 1994.

Greenwood, R., *Practising Community*, SPCK, London, 1996.

Greenwood, R., *The Ministry Team Handbook*, SPCK, London, 2000.

Greenwood, R., *Transforming Church: Liberating Structures for Ministry*, SPCK, London, 2002.

Greenwood, R., *Parish Priests: For the Sake of the Kingdom*, SPCK, London, 2009.

Greenwood, R., *Being Church: The Formation of Christian Community*, SPCK, 2013.

Greenwood, R. and Burgess, H., *Power: Changing Society and the Churches*, SPCK, London, 2005.

Gregory the Great: *Medieval Sourcebook: The Book of Pastoral Rule*, c. 590, in H. Davis, *Pastoral Care*, Paulist Press, New York, 1950.

Grint, K., *Leadership, Management and Command: Rethinking D-Day*, Macmillan, Basingstoke and New York, 2008.

Grint, K., *Leadership: A Very Short Introduction*, OUP, New York, 2010.

Grundy, M., *Understanding Congregations*, Continuum, London and New York, 1998.

Grundy, M., *What They Don't Teach You at Theological College*, Canterbury Press, Norwich, 2003.

Grundy, M., *What's New in Church Leadership?* Canterbury Press, Norwich, 2007.

Grundy, M., *Leadership and Oversight: New Models for Episcopal Ministry*, Continuum, London and New York, 2011.

Handy, C., *Understanding Organizations*, Penguin, London, 1976.

Handy, C., *Gods of Management*, Souvenir Press, 1978; Arrow, London, 1995.

Handy, C., *The Empty Raincoat*, Hutchinson, London, 1994.

Harle, T., *Embracing Chaos: Leadership Insights from Complexity Theory*, CPAS, Leadership Series L4, Grove, Cambridge, 2011.

Healy, N., *Church, World and Christian Life: Practical-Prophetic Ecclesiology*, CUP, Cambridge, 2000.

Hebblethwaite, P., *The New Inquisition: Schillebeeckx and Küng*, Collins, London, 1980.

Heywood, D., *Reimagining Ministry*, SCM, London, 2011.

Higginson, R., *Transforming Leadership: A Christian Approach to Management*, SPCK, London, 1996.

Holloway, R., *Dancing on the Edge: Faith in a Post-Christian Age*, Fount, 1997.

Howell, D., *Attlee*, Haus Publishing, London, 2006.

Hull, J., *Mission-Shaped Church: A Theological Response*, SCM, London, 2006.

Isaacson, W., *Steve Jobs: The Exclusive Biography*, Little, Brown, New York, 2011.

Jackson, M., *The Sociology of Religion*, Batsford, London, 1974.

Kasper, W., *Harvesting the Fruits: Basic Aspects of Faith in Ecumenical Dialogue*, Continuum, London and New York, 2009.

Küng, H., *The Church*, Search Press, London, 1968.

Küng, H., *Why Priests?* Collins, Fontana, London, 1972.

Küng, H., *On Being a Christian*, Collins, Fount, London, 1978.

Küng, H., *Disputed Truth: Memoirs*, Continuum, London and New York, 2008.

Kurtzman, J., *Common Purpose: How Great Leaders Get Organizations to Achieve the Extraordinary*, Jossey-Bass, San Francisco, 2010.

Lamdin, K., *Finding Your Leadership Style*, SPCK, London, 2012.

Lightfoot, J., *The Christian Ministry (In an added essay in St Paul's Epistle to the Philippians)*, Macmillan, London, 1869.

Ling, T. and Bentley, L. (eds), *Developing Faithful Ministers*, SCM, London, 2012.

Lovell, G., *Analysis and Design: A Handbook for Consultants in Church and Community Work*, Burns & Oates, London, 1994.

Lovell, G., *Consultancy, Ministry and Mission: A Handbook for Practitioners and Work Consultants in Christian Organizations*, Burns & Oates, London, 2000.

McAleese, M., *Quo Vadis? Collegiality in the Code of Canon Law*, Columba Press, Dublin, 2012.

McCaffry, T., *How to Become a Creative Church Leader*, Canterbury Press, Norwich, 2008.

Macquarrie, J., *Principles of Christian Theology*, SCM, London, 1966.

Martin, D., *A Sociology of English Religion*, Heinemann, London, 1967.

Martin, D., *A General Theory of Secularization*, Blackwell, Oxford, 1978.

Martin, D., *The Breaking of the Image: A Sociology of Christian Theory and Practice*, Blackwell, Oxford, 1980.

Messer, D., *Contemporary Images of Christian Ministry*, Abingdon, Nashville, 1989.

Migliore, D., *Faith Seeking Understanding: An Introduction to Christian Theology*, Eerdmans, Grand Rapids, MI, 2004.

Minear, P., *Images of the Church in the New Testament*, Lutterworth, London, 1961.

Moberley, R., *Ministerial Priesthood*, John Murray, London, 1897, 1907.

Moltmann, J., *The Crucified God*, SCM, London, 1974.

Moltmann, J., *The Church in the Power of the Spirit*, SCM, London, 1977, 1992.

Moltmann, J., *The Open Church: Invitation to a Messianic Lifestyle*, SCM, London, 1978.

Morgan, G. (ed.), *Beyond Method: Strategies for Social Research*, Sage, Newbury Park, CA, 1983.

Morgan, G., *Riding the Waves of Change*, Jossey-Bass, San Francisco, 1988.

Morgan, G., *Images of Organization: Of the Nature of Metaphor and its Importance in Organization and Management*, Sage, London, 1997, 2006.

Nash, S., Pimlott, J. and Nash, P., *Skills for Collaborative Ministry*, SPCK, 2008, 2011.

Nazir-Ali, M., *Shapes of the Church to Come*, Kingsway, London, 2001.

Nelson, J. (ed.), *Management and Ministry*, MODEM, Canterbury Press, Norwich, 1996.

Nelson, J. (ed.), *Leading, Managing, Ministering*, MODEM, Canterbury Press, Norwich, 1999.

Nelson, J. with Adair, J. (ed.), *Creative Church Leadership*, Canterbury Press, Norwich, 2004.

Newbigin, L., *The Gospel in a Pluralist Society*, SPCK, London, 1989.

Niebuhr, H. R., *Christ and Culture*, Harper, Torchbooks, New York, 1956.

O'Halloran, J., *Small Christian Communities: A Pastoral Companion*, Columba Press, Dublin, 1996.

Österlin, L., *The Churches of Northern Europe in Profile: A Thousand Years of Anglo-Nordic Relations*, Canterbury Press, Norwich, 1995.

Owen, D., *The Hubris Syndrome: Bush, Blair and the Intoxication of Power*, Politicos, Methuen, London, 2007.

Owen, D., *In Sickness and in Health: Illness in Heads of Government During the Last 100 Years*, Methuen, London, 2009.

Parsons, T., *The Social System*, Free Press of Glencoe, Collier-Macmillan, 1951.

Parsons, T., *Social Systems and the Evolution of Action Theory*, Free Press of Glencoe, New York, 1977.

Percy, M. and Nelstrop, L., *Evaluating Fresh Expressions: Explorations in Emerging Church*, Canterbury Press, Norwich, 2009.

Percy, M., *Shaping the Church: The Promise of Implicit Theology*, Ashgate, Aldershot, 2010.

Percy, M., *Anglicanism: Confidence, Commitment and Communion*, Ashgate, Farnham, 2013.

Peters, T. and Waterman, R., *In Search of Excellence: Lessons from America's Best-Run Companies*, Harper & Row, New York, 1982.

Peyton, N. and Gatrell, C., *Managing Clergy Lives: Obedience, Sacrifice, Intimacy*, Bloomsbury, T & T Clark, London, 2013.

Pickard, S., *Theological Foundations for Collaborative Ministry*, Ashgate, Aldershot, 2009.

Pickard, S., *Seeking the Church: An Introduction to Ecclesiology*, SCM, London, 2012.

Platten, S. (ed.), *Anglicanism and the Western Tradition*, Canterbury Press, Norwich, 2003.

Podmore, C., *Aspects of Anglican Identity*, CHP, London, 2005.

Polanyi, M., *Science, Faith and Society*, OUP/University of Chicago Press, 1946.

Pratt, A., *Practical Skills for Ministry*, SCM, London, 2010.

Prestige, G., *The Life of Charles Gore*, Heinemann, London, 1935.

Pritchard, J., *The Life and Work of a Priest*, SPCK, London, 2007.

Ramsey, A., *The Gospel and the Catholic Church*, Longmans, London, 1936.

Reed, B., *The Dynamics of Religion: Process and Movement in Christian Churches*, DLT, London, 1978.

Rien, R., *The Soul in Leadership*, Pastoral Series 102, Grove, Nottingham and Cambridge, 2005.

Roberts, R., *Religion, Theology and the Human Sciences*, CUP, Cambridge, 2002.

Roxburgh, A. and Romanuk, F., *The Missional Leader*, Jossey-Bass, San Francisco, 2010.

Rudge, P., *Management in the Church*, McGraw-Hill, Maidenhead, 1976.

Rudge, P., *Order and Disorder in Organizations*, CORAT, Australia, 1990.

Russell, A., *The Clerical Profession*, SPCK, London, 1980.

Saarinen, M., *The Life-Cycle of a Congregation*, Alban Institute, Washington, 1986, 2001.

Sanders, M. and Sanders, C., *Growing Benefices ... and How to Survive Them*, Diocese of St Edmundsbury and Ipswich Resources, 2013.

Savage, S. and Boyd-Macmillan, E., *The Human Face of Church*, Canterbury Press, Norwich, 2007.

Schillebeeckx, E., *Ministry: A Case for Change*, SCM, London, 1981.

Schillebeeckx, E., *The Church with a Human Face: A New and Expanded Theology of Ministry*, SCM, London, 1985.

Schön, D., *The Reflective Practitioner: How Professionals Think in Action*, Temple Smith, London, 1983.

Selby, P., *Be Longing: Challenge to a Tribal Church*, SPCK, London, 1991.

Selznick, P., *The Moral Commonwealth: Social Theory and the Promise of Community*, University of California Press, Berkeley, 1992.

Selznick, P., *Leadership in Administration: A Sociological Interpretation*, Harper, New York, 1996.

Senge, P., *The Fifth Discipline: The Art and Practice of the Learning Organization*, Random House, London, 1990.

Sørensen, E. and Torfing, J. (ed.), *Theories of Democratic Network Governance*, Palgrave Macmillan, London, 2008.

Stewart, A., *The Original Bishops: Office and Order in the First Christian Communities*, Baker Academic, New York, 2014.

Stillwell, V., *Priestless Parishes: The Baptized Leading the Baptized*, Thomas More, Texas, 2002.

Swinton, J. and Mowatt, H., *Practical Theology and Qualitative Research*, SCM, London, 2006.

Sykes, S., *The Integrity of Anglicanism*, Mowbray, London, 1978.

Sykes, S., *Power and Christian Theology*, Continuum, London and New York, 2006.

Sykes, S. and Booty, J. (eds), *The Study of Anglicanism*, SPCK, London, 1988.

Thompson, J. and Thompson, R., *Mindful Ministry: Creative Theological and Practical Perspectives*, SCM, London, 2012.

Thung, M., *The Precarious Organization: Sociological Explorations of the Church's Mission and Structure*, Mouton, The Hague, 1976.

Thurian, M., *Churches Respond to BEM*, WCC, Geneva, 1986.

Tillich, P., *Systematic Theology*, Vol. 2. James Nisbett, Welwyn, 1964.

Torrance, T., *Royal Priesthood: A Theology of Ordained Ministry*, T & T Clark, Edinburgh, 1999.

Troeltsch, E., *The Social Teachings of the Christian Churches*, tr. O. Wyon, John Knox Press, Louisville, KY, 1992.

Turnbull, M. and McFadyen, D., *The State of the Church and the Church of the State: Re-imagining the Church of England for our World Today*, DLT, London, 2012.

Turner, V., *Betwixt and Between: The Liminal Period in Rites de Passage, in The Forest of Symbols*, Cornell University Press, Ithaca, New York, 1967.

Turner, V. and Turner, E., *Image and Pilgrimage in Christian Culture*, Columbia University Press, Oxford, 1978.

Tustin, D., *A Bishop's Ministry: Reflections and Resources for Church Leadership*, Paragon Publishing, Rothersthorpe, 2013.

Warren, R., *Building Missionary Congregations*, Board of Mission Occasional Paper No. 4, CHP, London, 1995.

Warren, R., *Signs of Life: How Goes the Decade of Evangelism?* CHP, London, 1996.

Watts, F., Nye, R. and Savage, S., *Psychology for Christian Ministry*, Routledge, London & New York, 2002.

Western, S., *Leadership: A Critical Text*, Sage, London, 2008.

Wickham, E., *Church and People in an Industrial City*, Lutterworth, London, 1957.

Wright Mills, C., *The Sociological Imagination*, OUP, Oxford, 1959, 2000.

Index of Names and Subjects

Adair, J., 78, 79, 91, 94, 100, 101, 111, 114, 140, 153
Adie, M., 130, 153
Alban Institute, 77, 153, 160
Allen, R., 56–8, 67, 133, 153
Anglican-Methodist Conversations, 64, 65, 69
Anglican-Roman Catholic Dialogue, 66–5
Apostolicity, 65, 66, 68, 70, 71, 72, 137, 151, 152
ARCIC, 63, 69, 152
Augsburg Confession, 67
Avis, P., 63, 69, 152, 153, 159

Baptism, Eucharist and Ministry (BEM), 62, 64–9, 71, 161
Baptist Church, 46
Bede, the Venerable, 54, 154
Belbin, M., 79, 154
Benedictine spirituality, 123 –4
Bentley, L., 119, 158
Bernard of Clairvaux, 122
Blakely, C., 110, 118, 154
Boyd-Macmillan, E., 91, 97, 99, 112, 123, 154, 160

Café Church, 11
Carr, W., 94 –5, 154
Celtic spirituality, 124
Cherry, S., 99

Christian Association of Business Executives (CABE), 124
Church Growth Research Programme, 20
Church of Sweden, 67
Church Pastoral Aid Society (CPAS), 103
Coherence, 131
Collegiality, 43, 65, 70, 89, 90, 146, 151
CORAT, 92
Cornick, D., 27
Corrymeela Community, 124
Covey, S., 111, 112, 155
Create the future, viii, 29, 30, 47, 134
Croft, S., 88
Cross, S., 21

Dadswell, D., 106, 121, 131, 155
Davie, G., 63, 155
Day, J., 46
Default position of oversight, 108, 125, 126
Downs, T., 80, 95, 100, 155
Drane, J., 56, 87, 155
Dulles, A., 86, 95, 98, 155

Ecclestone, A., 3–6, 133, 155
Edmondson, C., 111, 155
Elephant in the room, 1

Elford, K., 29–31, 37, 67, 104, 134, 155
Entrepreneurial leader, 82, 84, 153
Episkope, 26, 27, 34, 40, 61–9, 71, 72, 81, 87, 88, 99, 102, 131, 135, 136, 137, 153

Faith in the Countryside, 56
Family secrets, 2, 14, 88, 133
Finney, J., 20
Fisher, J, 139
Friedman, E., 2
Furlong, M., 63, 88

Gibbs, E., 19
Greenwood, R., 87–8, 98, 103, 117
Gregory the Great, 54, 98
Group Ministry, 35
Grubb Institute, 99
Grundy, M., 88, 101, 115, 116, 126, 148, 153, 156, 157
Guitierrez, G., 122

Harle, T., 117
Handy, C., 77
Heroic leader, 23, 82, 83, 87
Hierarchy, 23, 34, 41, 44, 67, 81, 83, 86, 129
Higginson, R, 127 –8, 154
Howard, S., 110, 118, 154
Hubris, 23, 108, 128 –30, 159
Hull, J., 20, 157

Industrial Mission, 18, 136
Iona Community, 124
Intuitive face of oversight, 114, 115

Jackson, M., 18
Jobs, S., 116

Kasper, W., 68
Kairos moment, 110, 118
Koinonia, 64, 65 –68, 70, 71, 72, 137, 151
Küng, H., 89–91, 98, 157

Lambeth Quadrilateral, 66
Lamdin, K., 89, 158
Leader, lædan, 75
Liminality, 60–1, 115, 116, 136, 158
Ling, T., 119

Managerial leader, 84
Managing the present, 31, 34, 37, 44, 48, 55, 134
Martin, D., 22, 158
Metaphor, 88, 89, 93, 94, 96 –100, 138, 150, 158
Methodist Circuit System, 34
McAlese, M., 70, 158
McCaffry, A., 112, 158
McFadyen, D., 113
Messy Church, 10, 38
Ministry team, 69, 142
Mission, vii, 1, 6,17–21, 22, 23, 24, 29, 35, 37, 39, 44, 47, 48, 50, 53, 55, 56, 66, 67, 73, 88, 98, 102, 118, 127, 136, 142, 149
MODEM, 61, 117
Moltmann, J., 91, 158
Morgan, G., 21, 94, 158
Myers-Briggs personality-type indicator, 121

Nurture identity, 29, 30, 45, 93, 134

Osterlin, L., 63, 159
Owen, D., 129, 159

Paroikia, 54
Pastoral cycle, 119
Percy, M., 24, 28, 105, 159
Personal development face of
    oversight, 107, 108,120 138
Pickard, S., 81, 86
Podmore, C., 54, 159
Porvoo Common Statement, 63, 64
Price, P., 76, 120
Pritchard, J., 89, 159
Public face of oversight, 55, 107–9,
    138

Ramsey, M., 52–3, 113, 160
Rawsthorne, J, 148
Reed, B., 61, 160
Reflective practice, 115, 118, 122
Retired clergy, 1, 37, 40, 147
Roberts, R., 91–2, 160
Romanuk, F., 118
Roxburgh, A., 118, 160
Rudge, P., 92–3,134

Saarinen, M., 77–8
Sacks, J., 27, 59
Saunders, M. and C., 50
Savage, S., 91, 97, 99, 112, 1123
Schillebeeckx, E., 52, 90
Schön, D., 118
Second Vatican Council, 89, 90,
    134
Selby, P., 88
Senge, P., 25–6, 100
Sentamu, J., 76, 119
Sheffield Industrial Mission, 3
Shepherd, 7, 33, 60, 72, 96, 98,
    100, 110, 137, 148, 153
Sigmoid curve, 77
Social leader, 82, 85
Society of St Francis, 124

Stamp, G., 79, 94, 100, 101
Stevenson, K., 98
Sykes, S., 86, 92, 99, 160

Team, 1, 10, 12, 20, 23, 25, 26,
    34, 36, 38, 40, 71, 78, 79, 82,
    83, 94, 98, 104, 109, 111, 121,
    138, 147
Team leadership, 76, 79, 99, 114,
    142–3
Team ministry, 34, 45
Teamwork, 78
Theodore of Tarsus, 54
Thompson, J., and Thompson, R.,
    88, 99, 119
Thung, M., 19, 23–4, 43, 136, 161
Thurian, M., 62
Tiller, J., 36, 41
Tillich, P., 129–30, 161
Transition curve, 140
Turnbull, M., 113
Turner, V., 60
Tutu, D., 124

Unity, 65, 68

Visitation, 52, 58–60, 69, 136

Warren, R., 20, 161
Watching over, 7, 8, 26, 27, 105
Watching over one-another in
    community, 24, 27, 29, 64, 135,
    137, 139, 145
Watts, F., 91, 161
Wesley, J., 34
Western, S., 22–3, 161
Wickham, E., 55, 136, 161
Williams, R., 123–4, 127
Working as One Body, 92
Wozniac, S., 116